MODERN GERMAN AUTHORS
TEXTS AND CONTEXTS
Ed. R. W. Last

VOLUME TWO

ILSE AICHINGER

by

J. C. ALLDRIDGE

DUFOUR EDITIONS, INC.
Chester Springs, Pa.
1969

71-7?

MODERN GERMAN AUTHORS—Texts and Contexts
ed. R. W. Last

Volume One :   HANS ARP—the poet of Dadaism
by R. W. Last
with four illustrations

Forthcoming volumes :

PETER WEISS	by	*I. Hilton*
J. BOBROWSKI	by	*B. Keith-Smith*
PETER HANDKE	by	*N. Hern*
GOTTFRIED BENN	by	*J. M. Ritchie*

Library of Congress Catalog Number 74-92613

© Oswald Wolff (Publishers) Limited, London, 1969

MADE AND PRINTED IN GREAT BRITAIN BY
THE GARDEN CITY PRESS LIMITED
LETCHWORTH, HERTFORDSHIRE

CONTENTS

For Beatrix

'We are such stuff as dreams are made on . . .'
'This is fairy gold, boy, and 'twill prove so . . .'

Shakespeare

ESCARPMENT

For what would I do
if it were not for the hunters, my dreams,
who, in the morning,
descend on the other side of the mountains,
in the shadows.

Ilse Aichinger

I

INTRODUCTION

In a rare expression in public of any opinion of her own work, Ilse Aichinger said in 1952, when she received the annual prize of the 47 Group, that creative writing must not be virtuosity without risk, it must not be polished and filed to the neglect of the spirit. This statement can well serve as a guide to a study of her writings.

She published her first work some twenty years ago, long enough for it to be pertinent to try to assess her development and to determine whether her gain in stature as an author is commensurate with the increase in the volume of her works. Certain it is that her reputation has risen steadily. Her first work, the tremendously moving novel *The Greater Hope,* made a deep impression on those privileged to read it. The talk about this new young writer soon died down; little discussion followed. There was no general eager anticipation of further publications.

Slowly, and undeterred by lack of acclaim, she has continued to write, and often to publish a piece of creative writing long after its completion. None of her published works, whether poem, story or dialogue, has burst upon the scene; each has startled the public rather by its unobtrusiveness. One has often had the impression, when reading one of her works for the first time, of a silent figure, by whom one has been observed and of whose existence one has been unaware.

7

Here, then, is one factor common to all her works:
their silent appeal. They demand, if we are to understand them, a respectful approach, almost humility.
One at least of her stories remained unpublished for
twelve years after it was written. The effect on the
reader or audience is one of surprise that such gems
of sensitive understanding of the human spirit,
expressed in such precise language, should not have
attracted attention before.

Her style has not changed throughout her twenty
years of creative writing. Nor has she changed in
demanding a sustained effort from her readers to
apply other than the accepted modes of thought in
trying to understand her meaning. The underlying
theme has always been the same : man in the bondage
of his own unenlightenment, all too often one which
he accepts willingly or about which he is indifferent.
It is certain that this has never ceased to cause her
concern.

It is in the form of her works that a change in
Aichinger is noticed. From her first work, the only
novel she has published, she has moved through
short stories, a radio play, lyric poems, and the
dialogue, which is her special contribution to the
literature of the mid-century. In her latest publication
we have again short stories. In all her works the
reader's sympathy is sought in a language which uses
no histrionics, no extreme devices of syntax to
heighten its effect and to stress the meaning. Limitation of vocabulary to the experience of everyday life
and of persons of humble position enables Aichinger
to render her meaning and appeal direct.

Her biography is briefly told. She was born in
Vienna on November 1st, 1921. She grew up there

and in Linz, experiencing a normal childhood and schooldays until 1938. The *Anschluß* in March of that year caused a national upheaval and brought great difficulties for her and for her relations. The restrictions imposed upon her included refusal of permission to study at the university. It was only after the war that she was able to matriculate. During her two years as a student in the Faculty of Medicine she wrote *The Greater Hope*, which was published in 1948. Shortly after this she abandoned her studies and became in her native city permanent reader for her own publisher, S. Fischer Verlag.

A move to Ulm in Württemberg to collaborate in the founding and early work of the Academy for Design did not interrupt her work as reader for Fischer nor her own creative writing. For some years she has been a member, and an increasingly critical one, of the 47 Group.

This group of mostly young German writers met first in 1947 at the suggestion and invitation of the well-known critic, Hans Werner Richter. Its purpose was to try to find new directions for German writing, which had been debased and then stifled under the Nazi dictatorship. At its meetings selected writers read from their recent unpublished work for criticism and discussion by fellow writers and any other critics present. The Group, whose membership has increased considerably since 1947, from which year it gets its title, has met twice annually; in recent years some meetings have been held outside Germany. At each gathering a prize, agreed by majority vote, is offered for the best work read. Ilse Aichinger received this prize in 1952 for her story 'Oration under the Gallows'.

9

In the same year she received the Austrian State Prize for the Encouragement of Literature. Her continued literary activity has brought her three more awards: the Literary Prize of the City of Bremen in 1955, the Immermann Prize awarded by the City of Düsseldorf a year later and, in 1961, the Bavarian Literature Prize. She is a member of the Academy of Arts in Berlin and of the West German PEN Club. She is married to the German poet and writer of radio plays, Günter Eich, and they live now in her native land.

Like several other writers she has become increasingly critical of the complacency in some cultural circles and groups, and has recently collaborated with her sympathisers in drawing up and presenting manifestos against war, especially against the Vietnam War and its instigators.

2

PROSE, POETRY AND DIALOGUES

The range of Ilse Aichinger's work is wide. She began with a novel, and her next publication was a radio play. In between this and a second radio play published eight years later, she experimented with short stories, the earliest collection of which—*The Bound Man*—contains some of her most characteristic and important work. Concurrently with this there appeared a series of dialogues. Her subsequent publications in collected form are all prose stories. Scattered through various periodicals are some two dozen lyric poems, written at intervals throughout her creative period, and not yet collected separately in book form. A predominance of prose, at least in quantity, is evident.

Her novel is a remarkable piece of writing. It contains the germ of nearly all her subsequent work and themes are begun in it which are followed up in later writings. It tells the story of a group of children in a country overrun by the Nazis, who try by emigration to escape their threatened fate. The central figure is a half-Jewish girl, Ellen, through whose precocious eyes the stages of the sufferings of these and many other children are seen. At the end of the book Ellen is killed by an exploding shell. The martyrdom of these rejected and condemned children is seen under the symbolic sign of 'the greater hope' of salvation at the last minute and of redemption, in the biblical sense, so that 'all things work together for good in them that love God'.

Although the novel was not published until 1948, three years after the end of the war, its mood throughout is unquestionably that of war and its attendant conditions. She worked long at her novel, aware as she was writing of the effects of the German occupation of her country, and interpreting much of what she observed and experienced. She herself has obviously known surveillance, chicanery and even pursuit.

Ellen, for all her perspicacity, is yet young enough to feel and represent the mood and thoughts of her playmates. Their games seem natural enough; they are the conventional games of children everywhere, but here they are burdened with the weight of dire political circumstances: occupation by a hostile power and the consequent danger to the opponents of a newly-imposed and harsh regime. Under the guise of exploration and travel to far-distant lands, Ellen and her playmates rehearse plans for a mock emigration, which, in the course of the novel, proves to be deadly serious in the literal sense. As the reader will realise more and more later, the events are played out on two levels simultaneously, that of cruelly mocking reality and that of the dream.

The dream-element is not new, but in few contemporary authors is it so revealing of the true meaning of the story as in Aichinger's work. The hope of the hunted children, of Ellen and her young friends, to attain freedom by escape through emigration from the relentless occupying power would, on a more factual level, be so improbable that it alone could not sustain the reader's interest for the length of this novel. But it has other significances. The tension and the possibility are kept alive by the 'double' life the children lead; the half-preposterous hope of an exit visa is fanned and kept alive by the imaginative and 'parabolic' scenes of the children's games, re-enacting as they frequently do events from the New Testament. The attentive reader will often recognise parables in Aichinger's work.

The ten chapters of the novel are set in a wide variety of scenes reminiscent of Kafka—in offices, in darkened rooms, in attics and cellars, and gradually, as the climax is reached, in the parks and streets, amid the sounds and sights of battle. Chapter One, entitled 'The Great Hope', sets the picture of a persecuted people seeking to flee. Adults are unable to find a way and can offer only words as help and comfort. With the unerring and relentless realism of a child, Ellen tries to act as mediator. She succeeds in making her opponents understand her aims, but no practical solution is found and resignation to their fate seems to be the only outcome for the children. Again it is Ellen who offers some comfort and a possible solution in the thought that self-abnegation, building, through one's own sacrifice, a new world, a new faith and a new hope, is a satisfaction for the whole world, the 'greater hope' of the novel's title. 'Greater love hath no man than this . . .'

The juxtaposition throughout the work of a pitiless world writhing in the horrors of war and death, and a serener world of a soaring spirit, is most skilfully contrived. The imagery is by no means ethereal; often there occurs in the course of the story a report, a message couched in terse military or political language, often in the form of a telegram, but offering the material basis of a parable. The personification of night and darkness in Chapter Seven is a striking example :

> '. . . The night leaps down from heaven, . . . it is covering us up,' sighed the people. . . . The night shook with laughter, but silently, pressing warily both hands to her eyes and mouth. For her command was otherwise, and read : 'Leap down, uncover, reveal,' . . . and she revealed the pitilessness of the world.

Even more striking in its deeper significance is the winged dream in Chapter Eight, where the engine driver appears as a 'peaceful leader', who is forced by circumstances into the position of 'misleading', that is, through being compelled to drive passengers to a fateful destination, different from the one he and they desired. Here dream and reality almost converge. The conflict between the two individuals, driver and managing director, on practical issues reflects the deeper conflict of loyalties and purpose. It also throws light on the gulf separating the background and aims of Ellen and her friends from those of the occupying power. The whole conversation in this chapter illustrates contrasts and parallels on social, political and psychological levels. A possible way out is suggested by the driver :

> 'We must find a new route, we must build a new route, a strange, unknown one, one that nobody has hitherto traversed, a route without a terminus, the route which leads to our objective and destination.'

It is the same engine driver of whom it is said shortly afterwards that 'he had taken upon himself the supreme oblivion like a sudden recollection'.

This resistance is sharpened in outline and intensity in the interrogation scene later in the same chapter, where the rôle of the resistance fighter, the ally of Ellen and the other children, is taken over from the engine driver by the police clerk. This eerie scene takes on a deeper significance through the symbolic reference to the cherry tree. This tree, according to Celtic mythology, was noted for not being a 'pursuing' tree, that is, no weapons were made from its wood, unlike, for example, the oak or the yew. It was thus not a 'slighting' tree. It is interesting to note that it was at one time in the Early Christian Church connected wtih the Nativity story as related in St. Matthew's Gospel. Bibi, one of Ellen's playmates, rejects the idea of 'being' a cherry tree, thus declaring, in effect, her refusal to play a pacifist rôle. Ellen calls Bibi to task for this. Exasperating as Ellen's attitude may appear to readers today, it is at least consistent with Aichinger's purpose in showing these children as victims.

At the conclusion of the story we are able to marshal the salient facts. Ellen stands as a buffer between both sides : her mother has been driven out of the country and her father is a collaborator. Some children are sent to camps, and some are rescued by international organisations. Traitors and friends are almost indistinguishable; loudspeakers make administrative and political announcements to the population, and the secret police are everywhere. There are curfews, deportations, disappearances. Ellen and the other children play their games, and only Ellen has a deeper understanding of things.

Fantasy and reality are interwoven, a sign both of the true situation of the time and of Aichinger's frequent reference to dream. In both, the transition from certainty to uncertainty, from clear to unclear situations, is frequent and hardly discernible.

The short stories, whether consciously or unconsciously, treat again some of the themes of the novel, but confining each one within a separate framework.

In 'The Bound Man' Aichinger comes closest to Kafka. A man wakes to find himself bound up. He surveys his condition without anger, and, apparently, without surprise. After calmly reflecting on his material losses—money, shoes, knife, and so on—he discovers that his bonds allow scope for a certain degree of movement. The message is clear : we can do in our limited life much more than we often realise. This is emphasised later on in the story when the bound man himself takes the initiative, having realised his limitations, and he becomes the centre of attraction, actually offering something which helps the circus owner to extend the entertainment range of his circus. By realising our limitations, we can go far towards overcoming their restricting effects, and can thus develop our spiritual resources. The tension is increased when the idea is mooted of severing the bonds that bind the man. The circus owner and the man both fear this eventuality, but for different reasons. The circus owner sees in an unbound man a loss of attraction and therefore of income, and the bound man himself has grown so accustomed to his situation that complete freedom is now distasteful. He has come to accept his condition : 'In thy service is perfect freedom'. This state is the true freedom, that in which one has control over oneself. After he has killed the wolf, he moves even more uncertainly and when, in spite of all resistance, his bonds are released, he disintegrates completely.

'Life Story in Retrospect' offers an interesting development of the mirror theme met with so often in literature. Here the narcissism takes on a calmer, more objective tone, due only partly to the objectivity arising out of the girl's situation as a disembodied spirit, such as Keats envisaged. The overhung, clouded or blank mirror can do more than a normal reflecting mirror : it can make it possible for the beholder to do everything without memory or cognisance of external circumstances, thus enabling an avoidance of grief, as the relatives of the girl in this story discover. Everything is in the mirror, it is comfortingly stated, and in it one re-enacts all the things one wants to be forgiven for.

Equally remarkable in this story is the precision of events, especially the funeral, and the clarity of the view with which the girl sees in retrospect all the last events of her life and those which immediately followed. The mental and spiritual mirror has indeed clarified the insight so clouded in life. At the end of the story we are back at the beginning of an earthly life, all the stages of which have been relived and are seen again in the rarified light of the spirit. As T. S. Eliot put it :

> . . . in my end is my beginning, . . .
> in my beginning is my end.

The difference between the human beings in bondage in the story 'Lake Spirits' and the central figure in 'The Bound Man' is that the former have gone into bondage with their eyes open, if not willingly. Whereas the bound man wakes up to find himself in his predicament, the characters of these three thematically linked scenes in 'Lake Spirits' are seen to allow this condition to overtake them or to allow themselves to fall into it. Their attempts to keep alive while it is summer, a parable for this life, whatever means they adopt, are tolerably successful. Makebelieve and makeshift both help. But when summer draws to an end, when, that is, life draws to its close, these subterfuges will no longer do and each one of us, like the people in these three little scenes, is thrown back on something deeper. They are all pathetic, because they just have not got any reserves to stand them in good stead, least of all the sailor on the mail ferry.

The strange, almost whispered monologue 'Where I Live' centres round one individual's realisation of loss of contact, not only with her own world but with herself. A key word for the understanding of the story comes early on : she says she has not yet completed her removal into the flat, and may therefore be understood not yet to belong properly. This may offer a clue to her uncertainty in finding her right abode. Even the nameplate on the door is no longer a sure guide, and the constant wandering from storey to storey reflects the unendingness of her quest. Would it have been different, had she left the concert any earlier or later? At one moment we feel that she has succeeded in finding her abode, but a glimpse at the nameplate stirs doubts in her. Her thoughts on the morrow remind us of the woman with the sunglasses in 'Lake Spirits'.

The proximity of neighbours and even of her lodger, all practical people, serves only to underline her helplessness and indecision. They are all people who have confidence and no doubts and cannot understand her situation or problem—a theme which is repeated in at least one of her dialogues. As so often in life, these neighbours are either too shy or are incurious, and the stricken one has no other way open than to sink down and face even grimmer realities, symbolised here by final residence in the canal, where there are no windows and only the hope that one can at least sink no lower.

For all its natural anxiousness the mouse in the story of that title has, in spite of living in a circumscribed world, more certainty than most of the human beings which it observes from its peephole. It hesitates to come out for fear of being involved in, and probably swamped by, mankind's prevalent uncertainty and doubt. It maintains therefore an impartiality vis-à-vis the world, and we see at least one creature content and confident in the world it knows. Not for the mouse is the constant fear known to man that he might suddenly be transformed into a spirit or ghost and thus have to face himself and his own inner being, as Aichinger has written in one of her other stories 'The Advertising Hoarding'. 'No,' the mouse whispers comfortingly to itself, 'the sound of the ice breaking leaves me quite indifferent'; and the mouse remains impartial to laughter from outside. Comforted though it may feel at its simple philosophy, the reader remains disturbed that human beings can stay thus withdrawn from the world and refuse to face life and its hard blows. The skill with which Aichinger has shown us the minuteness of the mouse's world and its clear but narrow view intensifies our uneasiness at our own situation.

The last prose story included in this edition to illustrate Aichinger's range and viewpoint, 'My Green Donkey', contains several characteristics which mark her style and impact. Attention is drawn at once to the use of the adjective 'green', which occurs so frequently in her work and about which more will be said later in the present essay. Suffice it to say now that it epitomises for her a freshness, a hope, a tenderness. Then we notice that it is *her* donkey, not *any* donkey. This sound of possessiveness may strike at first an aggressive note, but will be understood later in the story to be the opposite. Lastly, why a donkey? In some way this creature is as reticent as the mouse just mentioned. In this story, as in 'Where I Live', the narrator herself shows reticence : 'I will not ask them where the donkey comes from, nor whose he is, nor where he goes to every day over the bridge.' And yet there is a care, a concern, even a tenderness in observing, recording and reporting every daily or regular passage of the donkey over the bridge, and about his comfort. Surprise is the donkey's most outstanding characteristic, the observer finds; it is also one which lends him distinction. The observer's tenderness becomes increasingly evident, and, in the decision not to pursue the donkey, not to track him down to his lair or stable, and to train herself for the day when he will pass over the bridge no more, she exhibits the self-sacrifice of genuine love, the true love which wants only the best for the loved one.

Ilse Aichinger has seemed to revive the age-old literary and philosophical genre, the dialogue, and to have added to it a quality which has made it peculiarly her own and particularly suited to her temperament and to her purpose. Very early, in the literature of Europe at least, it was usual to tell the pre-history or antecedents of a larger work. In spite of its original meaning of a conversation between two people, it included from very early times also conversations between more than two persons. Aichinger has followed this pattern; no more than about half her dialogues adhere strictly to the classical pattern.

A closer investigation of the later history of this form of literature will show how closely Aichinger has observed its tenets and followed its uses. For, in the Middle Ages (Petrarch), Humanism (Machiavelli), the eighteenth century (Berkeley) and even in the nineteenth century (Walter Pater and Hugo von Hofmannsthal) the Socratic method was followed when it was desired to throw light on a subject from different angles within a short space and time. The culmination of the development of this art form seemed to have been reached in the comic and satirical periodicals which proliferated so astonishingly freely in the nineteenth and early twentieth centuries. Ilse Aichinger has given it a new lease of life.

Her use of it follows the general Socratic pattern : either one individual tries to elicit information from another about a point of personal or mutual concern, or two or more like-minded individuals strive to solve a problem by discussion. Aichinger's dialogue 'First Term' is an example of the first type and the dialogue 'Sunday Duty' illustrates the second pattern. A third type has either an older or a wiser person guiding, advising or consoling one less so. The example of this type in the present edition is the dialogue 'Never at Any Time'. A typically Aichinger exception is 'Belvedere', where the whole conversation is a tour-de-force of failure in communication in the style Ionesco has made familiar.

It is, furthermore, an art form which suits her well. It requires economy of words and focuses attention narrowly on what is being said. Often the meaning runs on two different levels simultaneously. Misconstructions, one may think perhaps at times deliberately encouraged, are easily possible, a circumstance that contains a warning and demands our unremitting attention. Lastly, the dialogue is short, and in this it differs from the radio play, with which it has something in common, and out of which it may have developed. It concentrates on one theme, one point of view, one thought, plan or idea.

'Never at Any Time' is the attempt of a wiser and more far-sighted person (the dwarf) to persuade the materialist to think beyond the immediate cares of daily life and work. These entirely divergent attitudes are neatly emphasised, with Aichinger's wonderful economy of materials, by the reference to the fact that the dwarf looks continually out of the window and the student does not. We shall surely not be deluded by the dwarf's gentle clowning into believing that he is not serious. For the student has, by the very fact of his studies in marine engineering, fundamentally the intention of moving out into a wider world; it is just that he will not give this any thought now. Obsession with daily affairs, however essential in themselves, must be tempered with vision : this is the dwarf's urgent message. 'Between three and four' is his repeated admonition : the dwarf is always at his disposal, but the student must learn to see and choose the right moment. At the end, the reader also is faced with two views of time : strictly and literally 'temporal' time, and 'infinite' time.

A brief acquaintance with the physical situation of the Belvedere Palace in Vienna is a necessary background to the understanding of the dialogue 'Belvedere'. The Palace is in two parts connected by a sloping garden on the Versailles pattern. The Lower Palace is a little smaller than the upper part, which is the residence proper. The lower part was designed as an Orangery. The whole was presented by a grateful nation to Prince Eugene of Savoy for his distinguished services in finally ridding the country of the Turks at the Battle of Zenta in September 1697. The Palace has long been State property.

This dialogue is a sustained example of two practical and efficient people talking at cross purposes, getting deeper and deeper into the mire of misunderstanding through inability to see the other's standpoint. It is a situation which Aichinger suggests is common enough and which is even in danger of becoming worse through man's refusal to try to understand his fellows. The despair at the end is a poignant expression of our helplessness in the situation for which we must bear responsibility. Hope alone is not enough.

In considering what may seem to be a normal situation, that of a student looking for lodgings, we are struck by the very first words of the 'stage direction' in the dialogue 'First Term', and note that the student 'is no longer young'. We may, therefore, expect a slightly unusual conversation with undertones of deeper significance. We see a person seeking spiritual help in her venture into the unknown, at least a venture on to a higher spiritual plane. Her frequent references to her vicar at home reveal her uncertainty and her reliance on others. She cannot expect her interlocutor to know who he is, nor what significance the student places on his advice, even though she insists in the beginning on referring to him as a recommendation. Here, more than in any other of the dialogues included in the present edition, the reader is assisted by a study of the 'stage directions'. We have already mentioned the reference to the fact that the student is no longer young, a reference which arouses the reader's curiosity as much as any conventional statement or speech. When the porter is suddenly confronted with the student's rather puzzled allusion to the existence of the hostel in the telephone director, she, the porter, stands erect before delivering her rather ambiguous answer, ambiguous at least to the student : 'Open in the temporary sense of the word, but full up in the permanent sense.'

At the stage where they discuss the eternity of God, the student shows her nervousness by fiddling with her head-scarf, and the reader has an inkling that the whole conversation centres round life, and round death and eternal life, that the student is in fact on the threshhold of death, and we understand her hesitancy and her final withdrawal, even though her attitude is condemned theologically. The door to eternal life through death is always open; once this is passed, there is no return; one becomes a permanent 'resident'.

The dialogue entitled 'Sunday Duty' is more truly a dialogue in the strict sense than any other in Aichinger's work. Here more understanding is reached than in others. The full realisation of this does not come until almost the last words, when the stewardess remarks on the fact that the interlocutors have very much the same hours of duty, a fact which we do not feel is a mere coincidence.

As also in 'Never at any Time', there is a period of time defined in exact hours, during which a human soul may come to terms with itself; indeed, it must do so. The main difficulty is that one is always dependent to some extent on others, even if it is a matter of one's own salvation. Here, in 'Sunday Duty', the stewardess needs the active help of the doctor, not merely his sympathy. From three o'clock till six is all she needs in order to be able to restore the broken spirit which has necessitated her attendance at the clinic, and which will lead to her being able to pay her debt to life before she can really live.

The number of poems that Ilse Aichinger has published to date is too few to warrant a separate volume, and they appear scattered in several periodicals. Sixteen were included in the anthology *Where I Live,* published in 1954.

Even more than in her stories, her characteristics of ambiguity and extreme economy of phrase, together with intensity of expression, are exemplified in her poems. The strangeness and alarm of her stories and dialogues are more concentrated in the poems. The vision of an alien world, so different from the real one, is even more vivid.

Correspondence is thought of normally as an exchange; indeed, the German title of this poem has 'Exchange of Letters', and presupposes in real life a partnership and free exchange, a genuine two-way traffic of trust and comfort. But the idea that the mail might be delivered at night introduces at once a strange, discomforting, eerie element, even though the moon is often thought of as benevolent. If the mail were to be delivered at night, we should receive the opposite of comfort; the messages would be at the same time messengers, reminding us of death, since they would appear in ghostly attire, silent and challenging. The colon at the end of the third line is a division not only of the physical poem on the printed page; it is a division into two worlds. The apocalypse which intervenes at this stage makes the 'sickness' comprehensible. But there is hope for the stricken one, since the angels hover in the background.

In the poem entitled 'Instructions' the author insists that the solution to all our unfulfilled plans and hopes lies within us. It is of no use to turn to easier-sounding solutions. We each carry in ourselves our own salvation. In the first five lines the situation is stated : we listen to our desires and wishes but do nothing about them except seal off all real approach. When reading this poem, one cannot help thinking of the parable of the talents and the need to use our gifts, and not store them up. In the last lines there is the hint of warning that many of those outside may only appear to be our guide and helpers; their friendship cannot solve all our deepest problems for us.

3

THEMES AND IMAGES

A reading of all Ilse Aichinger's work leaves the impression of a range of images so wide they can appear bewildering. Their very diversity makes it seem at first as though no tidy and easily viewed classification is possible, and even the most ardent reader of her work may feel daunted by her range and diversity. But it requires little more than a cursory glance to see possible groupings and connections. Outstanding in the reader's mind will be the frequent reference to colours, especially green. Next, he will remark on the ubiquity of sea(s), lakes, boats, ships, students of marine engineering, and sometimes, but less often, shipwrecks. Dwarfs and other traditional fairytale figures fit easily into these two main images and themselves make up a clearly noticeable image-group, together with those traditional country figures who encounter dwarfs—gardeners, milkmaids, shepherds and the like.

We have already touched, in the mere reference to this diversity of image, on elements of both the real and the imaginary world. As we review all her stories and dialogues, we shall gradually become aware of the preponderence of the dream as a background to much of her writings. Thus it is no longer possible to apply ordinary standards of judgement in assessing and attempting to understand and explain much of her work, where dream and reality veil each other to such a large extent. A new awareness of the bridge between reality and unreality, which we shall need to develop, will also stand us in good stead when we consider another of Aichinger's characteristics : namely, her strong religious sense. Angels, of course, are also very much part of the dream world, and play an important rôle in it. Night, thought of as an approach to the shades of death, the transitoriness of all individual life, the tolling of bells and concern for a state beyond the immediate, the present, and the obvious, including the awareness of guilt and sacrifice : all are an extension of this interest. In her treatment of the last named theme she comes very close to Kafka.

But, even after some realisation of the import of these diverse images has been achieved it still demands a special effort to grasp her manner of presentation. Here, in the truest sense, is an original writer. The diversity of themes and images is matched by diversity of presentation. Any one approach, in a specific story or dialogue, is not necessarily repeated in others. We find ourselves at times on the level of the real world and then suddenly in an entirely different realm, whether it be that of the dream or the spirit. And so the reader is gradually forced to take the dream world as a guide and standard for approaching and understanding these uniquely sensitive writings.

A preliminary word of caution must be given: dreams are not isolated phenomena but products of the human brain. Recent surveys of the setting of dreams show that the majority occur in places where human beings normally spend little of their waking life. Hence bedrooms, stairways, basements, bathrooms, entrance halls, cars, carriages, and boats preponderate. One's place of work, one's office, classroom or factory are seldom the setting. It is no easy matter to apply this to Aichinger's work. It is true that ships and sea settings are common in her work, and much that is connected with them. In this, and in her use of the hall and stairway as scenes for her stories, she follows a pattern observed in many dreams. Indeed, her story 'Where I Live' is set almost entirely in the hallway of a block of flats. There is no reference in Aichinger to places of entertainment, so common in dreams.

But she departs from the commonly observed 'dream scene pattern', in her reference to occupations, as distinct from representatives of a particular occupation, and here she is already in the realm of the fairytale, where, for example, there is no household drudgery mentioned, even though the inferences are common enough (clean house, bread already baked, etc.). The commonly observed fairytale phenomena, the simple juxtaposition of good and bad, happy and unhappy, and similar basic emotive reactions, are modified in Aichinger by her own impassiveness and restraint. If we accept that dreams are not random images but rather collections of images, and that what they contain and do not contain conforms to definite patterns set in the context of the life and problems of the individual dreamer, we shall be able to learn something of the mainsprings of her imagination.

A first step towards a consideration of symbols in dreams is the realisation that many of the frequent images which are treated in the interpretation of dreams, such as nudity, and missing trains, do not occur in Aichinger or are not preponderant in her work. Fantasy is not subject to the logical rules which govern real objects and situations. The fantasy is an intensely private experience and yet it is vivid to the beholder when revealed. It is a compensation for inadequacy, a regulator of life. Wishes expressed in dreams are those one usually wants to hide. Rewards sought are usually those denied one, and fears are those too grim to be confronted. All images employed in fantasy are symbolic.

Symbolism is the subjective means whereby man organises his objective experience of life; the inner emotions are fused with the environmental perception. Upon this fusion memory is stored up and becomes the source from which dreams develop and emerge. The imagery of dreams is often visual in Aichinger and frequently has reference to colour. It has been suggested that colour dreams are extremely rare, and their comparative frequency in Aichinger's work warrants some consideration of the subject here.

Traditionally colours have had associations with, amongst other things, days of the week, months of the year, seasons, nationalities and numbers. Edith Sitwell created a character Emily, who was associated in the mind of her creator with coloured primulas; this concept, along with Aichinger's preoccupation with green and with numbers, is not very far from Galton's theory of visualised numerals. But an even more interesting and significant philosophical and psychological background to the study of colours is to be found in the works of Jakob Böhme, who announced a theory of light and quarternity in 1620. In this theory, green is associated with liberty and the promise of the kingdom of glory for the reborn soul. It is a world in which blue also plays a part. The reader of Aichinger will be immediately reminded of the frequent occurrence of green and blue in her work. The reference to blue in Böhme's writings finds a touching echo in several of Aichinger's works, especially in the story 'Life Story in Retrospect', where the girl is described as at one stage hanging up her blue school uniform cap.

The colours blue and green have their own brightness, demonstrating the alchemic duality of *corpus* and *spiritus*; add to this the *anima* and there can be seen immediately a bridge between the alchemy of the Middle Ages, the mysticism of the seventeenth century and the psychoanalytic *anima* of Jung.

The reference to the colour green is frequent but it is rarely referred to as bright. It is evident that this colour has a special significance in her work, which is nevertheless not entirely subjective. She is in her writings seldom aware of shades of green. Good examples of her use of green are to be found in the story 'My green Donkey', and in the dialogue 'Never at any Time'. In this dialogue the dwarf represents knowledge, reflection and insight on the one hand, and, on the other, the moral qualities of goodwill and helpfulness to one's fellow men. Almost the first words the dwarf addresses to the student contain the enigmatical phrase: 'I compare various shades of green', and he adds that this is a never-ending preoccupation.

From Jung we learn that the archetype is an auto-nomous content of the unconscious. The fairytale often concretises the archetypes; characters in fairy-tale dreams appear in very much the same way as happiness occurs in contemporary dreams. In these dreams ordinary, 'prototype' countryside phenomena such as cottages, food, and country people are all green; this is not surprising when we recall that the vegetable numen reigns in the woods. In Shakespeare's *Merry Wives of Windsor* there were green fairies (Act V, Sc. 5). This gives the connection, via pixies, with water; and from there a relation to the unconscious. It is necessary only to recall the very frequent references to water in all literature, especially as a means of suicide. The vegetable numen is often expressed via wood or water symbols, and Aichinger, in her frequent use of these, is in part following Böhme, for whom water represented the eternal essence of nature. Even in modern scientific enquiry, green has been statistically correlated with the sensa-tion function.

Other senses are involved in Aichinger's stories. The reader will recall references to sound (the frequency of bell ringing is remarkable), taste and touch. Every dream image is linked to a distinct feel-ing or group of feelings; this fact throws some import-ant light on 'Life Story in Retrospect'. Here the long, eternal sleep is symbolical of extreme loneliness, a sense in spiritual terms, as the angel in her works is symbolic of the messenger, a mental vision.

Almost more remarkable, even if only because it is so seldom met with, is the number symbolism which is found in her work. The dwarf in 'Never at any Time' insists on the student noting the critical period 'between three and four'; and the stewardess in 'Sunday Duty' reiterates her need for three hours only, namely from three till six. Both include the figure 'four', which Jung found to indicate a tendency towards integration. In all civilisations, in different cultures and on different levels of culture, from different societies and different groups or strata of society, amongst different races, climes and continents, similar dream symbols are found. Striking examples which come readily to mind are the reference to teeth in the 'Song of Solomon', which are likened to a flock of sheep, and the snake-being, symbol of the phallus. Jung's theory of the collective unconscious is concerned, amongst other things, with a number of fundamental symbols; common are the circle, the cross, the trinity, and the wise old man, so common in fairytale who appears in the dialogue 'Never at any Time' in the figure of a dwarf. This same theory also takes account of the sensation in dreaming of tramping upstairs, often accompanied by heart palpitations. Here it is possible to see some connection between Poe's story 'A Tell-Tale Heart' and Aichinger's 'Where I Live'.

Other common symbols in Aichinger are persons on the point of death or having just died ('Life Story in Retrospect'), the sensations of floating or flying, very closely connected with the state immediately preceding death (the frequency of reference to angels in Aichinger's stories and dialogues is pertinent here), a subject on which Havelock Ellis had much of great interest to say. Especially in Aichinger's latest publication, the collection of stories entitled 'Eliza, Eliza', there are many references to the skin and sensory obtuseness, to hysterical ecstasy with its reminder of

. .

primitive dance. The fan dance of the children in the story 'Eliza, Eliza' would be macabre, were it not for their innocence. It is a short step from here to music, especially to Bach, in some of whose work there is a clear association between dark colours (for example, blue, common in Aichinger) and low notes, inducing or inferring sombre feelings; and high musical notes are reminiscent of light colours (for example, green, also common in Aichinger) and happiness.

It is possible to assess in general terms the significance of dreams in Aichinger's work, assuming that an understanding of dreams does provide the most likely key to her meaning. If a 'coherent' dream were remembered and set out in all its detail, it is sometimes said, it would be tantamount to the actually experienced fevers of an incurable disease, such as Robert Louis Stevenson saw in the drawings of the architect Piranesi. Jung always insisted that dreams are not a neurotic symptom, but an objective product of the psyche, and thus best understood in series rather than in isolation. To bring Aichinger into relation with this assessment, it is necessary only to recall her theme of crossing the frontier, most clearly stated in her novel. Aichinger sees this crossing as a decisive step by the individual, at least in intention, indicating his will to achieve something.

This is not invalidated, even when the decisive step may appear to be one back towards one's origins. In Aichinger's story 'Where I Live' doors and rooms appear to be half open, into which an occasional glimpse may be had, even by the rightful inhabitants. These are chance glances, and often the room and its contents are not recognised. The reader is reminded of Jung's theory concerning the archetypes and the anima concept. In this same story the first person narrator finds herself in the end quite content to live in the cellar, which is reminiscent of the vessel, the hollow, the womb.

In all her writings the reader has the impression of a deeply religious woman, whose concern for the human spirit is expressed sometimes in Biblical terms and allusions, and sometimes in more general terms of Christian thought. Her novel bears witness to her concern towards those persecuted for their religion. Chapter Four contains direct references to many figures and scenes in the Bible—the Four Riders of the Apocalypse, Noah and the Ark, and, more indirectly, the Crucifixion.

The theme of guilt and atonement in the story 'The Bound Man' is a clear reference to the Old Testament; the belief in eternal life, and man's hesitant acceptance of this belief, lies at the heart of the dialogue 'First Term'. Nowhere do we read of a concession to standards lower than those of the Christian faith nor to a condoning of the ways of a permissive society such as has grown up in the years of Aichinger's literary development. Compassion, a recurring element in her thinking and in her attitude to her fellows, stands clearly expressed through all the different symbols and images in her writings.

4

STYLE AND LANGUAGE

Fairytale and folklore condition Aichinger's language, and elements of the collective unconscious are the source of many of her themes and much of her imagery. In her writing she has produced a verbal pattern of unusual force in contemporary German literature. Even in so simply constructed a piece of writing as a dialogue, the linguistic skill of the author poses in a very few pages a deep human problem. In 'Belvedere', for example, the reference to the esoteric activities of the herdsmen caring for the animals it is proposed should be accommodated in the gardens, and to their general well-being, stands in clear contrast to the official conversation, which is felt as a kind of undercurrent to the preoccupation of the Director of the Zoo. It strikes the reader as even stranger, since the two men attempt to conduct a purposeful conversation in a modern office, against a background of present-day governmental conditions. The reader, like the unfortunate Director of the Art Gallery, is non-plussed by the mixture of thrustful, insensitive bargaining and by the sense of being over-powered by a superhuman force.

An equally powerful contrast, though set on a humbler level, is shown in the dialogue 'Never at any time'. The homeliness of the student's room with its manually operated stove and the attendant pile of wood, the little book box instead of the more modern bookshelves, so reminiscent of Scottish students in the past whose main sustenance consisted of a bag of oatmeal in the corner of the room : all these contrast so strongly with the reality of the student's subject of study : marine engineering.

Much of this kind of contrast in Aichinger's work centres round animals. In the two stories 'The Mouse' and 'My Green Donkey' the narrator is absorbed in a consideration of the animal, but not in the 'scien-

35

tific' manner of the Zoo Director in the dialogue
'Belvedere'; this is a more individual preoccupation,
bordering on a self-identification. This kind of consideration is very evident in 'My Green Donkey',
where it entirely conditions the language. Out of the
frequent and regular transfer from the personal concern for the animal and its material needs to the
impersonal observation of its surroundings, there
evolves a language at once simple, slightly archaic,
and yet realistic :

> But how does he come, where does he come from,
> where does he originate from? Has he a mother
> or a bed of hay in one of the silent farms over
> there? Or does he live in one of the former offices
> where he has his own corner or piece of wall?

This impression is even more enduring in the story
'The Mouse', perhaps because of the unusually
restricted point of view the creature is forced to take.
Only one so near to other small creatures could be
concerned to note duck footsteps :

> I can hear steps everywhere : the steps of human
> beings, of ducks, of sleepwalkers, of sons and
> daughters, there are many steps, even those of the
> just, I can distinguish them all easily.

Only a creature so lowly can be in a position to sense
many possible directions within a confined space :

> . . . but the neighbours' children call out to me
> joyfully, and I catch the smell of them in my
> nostrils.

Even within the confined space the fantasy is free
and the catalogue of the mouse's imaginings is

couched in a language at once strange to us and reminiscent of a human past :

> ... or the mushroom gatherers, whose steps and talk I often hear, even if joylessly. And the pilgrims, everybody.

Even when divorced from specific context such as those outlined above, Aichinger's language still has an arresting quality. More obviously in the German original than in translation, her use of tense, her subtle shades of meaning lend much force to her writing and vividness to her message. Three examples are offered.

In 'Life Story in Retrospect', the dead girl's reflections on her past and her imagined observations of the domestic and official arrangements connected with her funeral gain immensely in poignancy through the author's use of the present tense. Not only is the almost unbearable tension of the girl's progress through these obsequies thereby maintained; it is heightened also for the reader, since he thus feels actually by her side in the dual capacity of observer and sympathiser :

> Your hearse waits at the crossroads for the green light. The rain has slackened. Rain-drops dance on the roof of the car. One can smell the hay in the distance.

The story 'Lake Spirits' is written mainly in the past tense. This affords the reader the necessary distance to understand the full import of the dilemma of the vicitims : for this is how the reader thinks of them; they are victims of their own inability to see or move outside their own human frailty. We share the author's sympathy with them and their loneliness

37

in a bond which she herself has forged for us and all humanity :

> With the cooler weather his friends left, and his children too returned to the town and school began. . . .
>
> . . . The boat began to rock and the sailor seized the opportunity to show the girls what he was worth. In his oilskin he climbed more often than was necessary over the railing, round on the outside and back again. In doing so, he slipped on the wet wood, since it had begun to rain even harder, and fell into the lake. And because he had one thing in common with sailors on ocean steamers, namely that he could not swim, and because the lake had that in common with the open sea, namely that one can drown in it, he drowned.

In all three scenes in this story this sympathy is underlined by a sudden change, also between present and future tense.

The even tenor of the events of the story 'Where I Live' is interrupted by a rhetorical remark or sometimes a question in the subjunctive, reminding the reader of the precarious situation of the flat-dweller and her dilemma :

> On the third floor I am usually overcome by a kind of exhaustion, which sometimes is so excessive that I feel as though I had already gone up four flights of stairs. . . .
>
> . . . I wonder, too, what would have happened if I had left the concert before it had ended. . . .
>
> . . . I have no reason to go to the caretaker for that, even less because of the view. He could quite

rightly say that a view is no part of a flat; the rent
is charged according to the size, not according to
the view. He could perfectly well tell me that the
view is my own affair.

These last words are indeed a convenient summary
of a dilemma met with commonly in Aichinger's
situations and characters.

Aichinger's narrative method deserves some attention. It might perhaps be more accurate to speak of
her narrative methods, since she displays a surprising virtuosity, when one considers the conditions
imposed by the folklore element in her stories and
dialogues. They do not restrict or mitigate against
the wide range of scene and plan in her work. Perhaps because of her close association in mind and
spirit with the dream world, she shows to a remarkable extent the facility to follow simultaneously
several narrative and thought threads in any one piece
of work. This is evident even where the time sequence
is scrupulously observed. Here again 'Life Story in
Retrospect' provides convenient examples. The open-
ing paragraphs put the reader at once on two time
levels : the girl's present state reviewing life from the
Beyond alternates with the immediate preoccupations
of those responsible for the administrative arrangements of the obsequies. And yet, such is her personal
integrity that the reader never feels himself forcibly
transposed from one world, or one should say from
one world level, to another and back.

In the story 'My Green Donkey', the narrator's
reflections range continually from a present preoccupation with the donkey, the object of her absorbed
attention, to a past consideration of his physical

39

comfort, and a thought about their possible future relationship. And yet the reader has almost on every line the feeling of being in the observer's vantage post and of trotting along over the railway bridge with the donkey.

Such examples occur in almost every story and could be multiplied as often as one mentions one of her stories. Yet the reader is never confused, even though the author appears at times to lose the thread of the argument or story, and even when she appears to concentrate on mental concepts. The apparent digression on the thoughts of the mushroom gatherers in 'The Mouse' illustrates this. The careful reader of Aichinger will not be deterred by such apparent digressions and will discern even in them the main thread of the story.

The unexpected shifts of emphasis which slide almost imperceptibly from one level to another, and even from one theme to another within a story, are characteristics which occur in all her work, and which set her apart from her contemporaries. We have seen pertinent examples in the story 'Life Story in Retrospect'. Less obvious are the examples in the dialogues. Amongst these 'First Term' is a convenient one for examination. Here, the alternation between matter-of-fact conversation about accommodation and the entirely unexpected reminiscence of a theology seminar, between this and such mundane matters as the travelling time from the student's home to the university and back again, is heavily charged with symbolism and remind the reader of Aichinger's constant preoccupation with more than one level of human existence, spiritual as well as physical; and the language, simple at first acquaintance, is full of double meanings.

In her use of metaphor her originality is equally evident. Her novel *The Greater Hope* is full of examples of her very personal use of this device. But also in her lesser works, in her poems in particular, there is no lack of it. Here she shows a remarkable affinity with her husband, Günter Eich. In 'Winter Answer', the first of the poems included in the present volume, we recover only slowly from the startling metaphor of a human being *tasting* grass :

> Grandmother, where have your lips gone,
> to taste for us the grasses . . .

The language of this poem is further remarkable for the clear impression it gives of mankind sensing the seasons and natural phenomena by more than the usual means of eye and scent.

Birds occur frequently in her poetry (and in that of her husband). In hers they are always of the opalescent or irridescent kind and the poems where they are mentioned are consequently lit up by the flash of a brightly-coloured word or by the sound of a whirring word, reminiscent of a bird's flight, as here, in 'Walk' :

> . . . the magpies start up behind your sheds
> and plunge down again with glittering wings into
> the shining pond . . .

The magnetic effect on the beholder of all these jays and magpies goes deeper than the mere visual flash; vocabulary does double duty. The association in her lines with what is bearable and understandable must be considered against a background of staircases and marshes, of dreams in the shape of mountains. The poem 'Escarpment' at the head of this essay is an illustration of this. There the language has a boldness matched by the boldness of the imagery. In the poem 'Dedication' the metaphor of the woollen hearts emphasises the indecision and uncertainty pervading the whole being and nature of the speakers. The mixed image in the next line is then no longer startling.

Aichinger's treatment of dialogue within her stories, as distinct from the dialogue as a separate genre, throws into relief her skill in maintaining at one and the same time on more than one level a train of events or thoughts. Most commonly this takes the form of a soliloquy conducted on different levels, a kind of mental ventriloquism. This may be illustrated by the following short extract from Chapter One of *The Greater Hope*, in which Ellen imagines a conversation between her mother and the shopkeeper while the mother is doing some hurried shopping, having left Ellen alone in the house :

But there was something wrong with this spring morning. Perhaps—perhaps it was autumn. And perhaps evening was drawing on.

All the better. Ellen was in complete agreement. At all events her mother had gone shopping. To the greengrocer's, just round the corner.

I must hurry, you know. Ellen is alone in the house, and one never knows what might happen. I should like some apples, please. I shall roast them, Ellen likes them like that best, and I've promised her that I'll make a little fire, since it's already getting cold. How much is that, please?

What? *How* much? No, that's *far* too dear. *Far* too much.

Ellen sat right up in bed.

A second method of fixing the reader's mind on more than one level of a story simultaneously is Aichinger's habit of transferring images. One effect of this is that it also enables her to economise with vocabulary to a large extent. At the beginning of Chapter Four of *The Greater Hope* there is a scene of brilliant imagery and at the same time economy of words:

> In the middle of the alley-way a red exercise book lay on the grey pavement, a vocabulary notebook for English lessons. Some child must have lost it; the storm fluttered the leaves. When the first rain drop fell, it fell on the red underlining. And the red underlining in the middle of the page overflowed its banks. Horrified, the meaning of the word overflowed on both sides and called out to a ferryman: 'set me over on the other side'.

This has added force in the German original through the double meaning of the last verb, incorporating the idea of translation from one language to another. It is a word-play startling in its simplicity and intensity, as becomes evident when one reads a little further:

> Translate, to set across a wide, deep river, and at that moment one does not see the banks. Set across, nevertheless, put yourself over and the others and the whole world. At all points on the shore there wanders lost the rejected meaning of the phrase: put me over, set me across. Help him,

bring him across. Why does one learn English?
Why didn't you ask him that before?

Arresting images and metaphors notwithstanding,
her vocabulary is simple, free from sententiousness
and always suited to the scene and setting. It is hardly
ever necessary to consult a dictionary when reading
her works, but rather those tracks of the mind which
are seldom explored. Her appeal is to a humanity
deep within each of us, addressed in a language
unadorned by flourishes and unadorned by experi-
ments in usage. Instead, the reader is held to a
consideration of such important differences as, for
example, those between 'see' and 'observe', between
'hear' and 'listen'.

Much of the impression and effect that her writing
has had on her contemporaries is recorded in the
opinions and summaries of critics and authors present
at the gatherings of the 47 Group. At various times
since 1951, three years after the publication of her
first work, and when she received for the first time
more than just passing attention, one critic noted
three outstanding characteristics of her writing. It was,
first, most evident that she owes much to Kafka, an
opinion which has been repeated ever since by all
critics and observers of her particular style, and which
is manifestly the most outstanding element in her
work. Secondly, her work has a marked lyric content.
Lastly, it is built up on a parabolic conception. So
much did she remind one fellow writer of Kafka that
he was guilty of a slip of the tongue in once referring
to her as 'Miss Kaf—, I *beg* your pardon, Miss
Aichinger!' These predominantly German views of
her and her work are fully shared by well-informed

French and English readers, insofar as they have left any record of their impressions.

Only in 1957, when she published her first dialogues, were she and her work discussed more often and in wider circles. These discussions revealed other characteristics of her work, during which it seemed to be agreed that it is enigmatical, surrealist, dissonant. Indeed, one reviewer has likened her style to the music of Alban Berg, with its 'sweet dissonances'. Some observers have welcomed her departure from that very common form of writing in post-war West Germany known as *Trümmerliteratur*, literature of ruins, bomb-damage literature. Another contemporary praises her 'unreal tales of overwhelming reality' (Rolf Schroers). Many have been fascinated by the dreamlike quality and yet sureness of her prose. Russian critics agree that her work is deep, and they wonder if many of her readers are able to read between the lines of her stories and dialogues. It is interesting to note that, at all the meetings of the 47 Group which Ilse Aichinger has attended, a fellow writer and critic, Wolfdietrich Schnurre, observed the contrast between the enthusiastic and uncritical acceptance of her readings by non-writers, and the equally enthusiastic but very critical reception accorded them by her fellow writers. Perhaps this is the real clue to the understanding of her work.

TRANSLATIONS

STORIES

THE BOUND MAN

The sun was shining when he awoke. Its light fell
on his face, so strongly that he had to close his eyes
again; the light streamed unhindered down the slope,
gathered in the streams, drawing with it swarms of
gnats which whizzed low over his forehead, encircled
it, trying to land but being continually overtaken by
new swarms. When he tried to brush them away, he
noticed that he was bound. A thin interwoven thread
cut into his arms. He let his arms fall back, opened
his eyes again and looked down at himself. His legs
were tightly bound as far up as the thighs and the
same cord was wound round his ankles, moved on
again criss-cross upwards and encompassed his hips,
his chest and his arms. He could not see where the
ends were knotted, and so he thought that the bonds
were faultless, without the slightest sign of fear or
hate, until he discovered that they left some free
play between his legs and ran almost loosely around
his body. They allowed even his arms free play and
had not bound them to his body but merely to each
other. This made him smile and for a moment he
had the idea that some children must have been
having a joke with him.

He stretched out for his knife but again the cord
cut lightly into his flesh. He tried once again with
greater care to reach into his pocket, and found it
empty. In addition to the little money that he had

possessed, his knife and his coat were missing. They had taken his shoes from his feet. He wetted his lips and tasted blood which had run down from his temples over his cheeks and chin and neck down into his shirt. His eyes hurt; when he left them open for a time, he saw the sky reflected as red strips.

He decided to get up. He drew in his knees as far as he could, put his hands on the fresh grass and sprang up. A flowering elder branch grazed his cheek, the sun dazzled him and the cords cut into his flesh. Half senseless with pain he sank back down again and tried once more. He went on doing this until the blood trickled out of the by now hidden cords. Then he lay still again for a long time and let the sun and gnats have their way.

When he woke up for the second time, the shade of the elder bush had already fallen across him and the stored-up coolness streamed out down through its branches. He must have had a blow on the head. And then they had laid him down here, like mothers lay their infants carefully under the bushes when they go into the fields. Their scorn and derision was not to be wasted.

The cords allowed him all kinds of movement. He propped himself up on his elbows and surveyed the play of the cord. As soon as it stretched taut he gave in, and then tried again, much more carefully. If he had got as far as the branches above him, he would have drawn himself up by them, but he did not reach them. He let his head fall back on to the grass, rolled over and got on to his knees. Groping cautiously with his feet, he suddenly stood up almost without effort.

A short distance away from him the pathway ran

across the plateau, where campions and thistles were flowering in the grass. He lifted a foot to tread them underfoot, but was prevented by the cord by which his ankles were bound. He looked down at himself.

The cord was knotted at the ankles but was interwoven in a playful kind of pattern. He bent down carefully and reached out to loosen it, but, however loose it seemed, it could not be loosened any more. In order not to have to tread on the thistles with bare feet, he pushed himself off the ground a little and hopped away over them like a bird.

A twig snapped and he stopped. Someone in the immediate neighbourhood managed only with an effort to restrain his laughter. The thought that he might not be in the position to defend himself as usual frightened him. He hopped on a little further until he was standing on the pathway. Far below him stretched shining fields. He could see nothing of the nearest village, and it would be night before he reached it, if he did not succeed in moving faster.

He tried to walk and noticed that the cord allowed him to put one foot in front of the other, if he raised each foot only a certain distance from the ground and put it down again before he had taken a full stride. It allowed him to swing his arms to the same extent.

He had not taken many steps before he fell. He lay across the pathway, watching the dust rise. He expected to hear the long suppressed laughter break out again, but all was silent. He was alone. When the dust settled, he rose and walked on. He looked down and watched the cord swinging as it dragged along, stretched slightly above ground and fell back again.

When the first glow-worms appeared, he succeeded in taking his gaze off the ground. He felt again that he was in its power, and his impatience to reach the next village gradually lessened.

He felt light-headed with hunger, and it seemed to him that he had reached a speed at which no motorcycle could have overtaken him. Or sometimes he stood his ground, and the earth came up towards him like a swift current to one swimming against the tide. The swift current bore along with it branches bent southwards by the north wind, young, stunted trees and lumps of turf with long-stemmed plants still growing out of them. The torrent finally swamped both branches and young trees until there was nothing above it but the sky and the man. The moon had risen and illuminated the open vault of the plateau, the pathway overgrown with short grass, the bound man walking along it with quick, restricted steps, and two hares crossing the hill just ahead of him who were lost to view beyond the slope. Although it was still cold at night at this season, the bound man lay down before midnight by the edge of the slope and slept.

In the morning light the animal trainer, who was encamped on the meadow with his circus near the village, noticed the bound man coming along the pathway, his gaze fixed pensively on the ground. He saw him stop and reach down at something. He bent his knee sideways, holding his arm outstretched to keep his balance, and with the other picked up an empty wine bottle from the ground, stood erect again and waved it above his head. He moved slowly in order to avoid being cut by the cord again, but to the circus owner it seemed like the voluntary limitation of a high speed. The indescribable charm of the movement delighted him, and while the bound man

looked round for a stone, on which to smash the
bottle, so that he could use the jagged neck to cut
the cord, the animal trainer came across the meadow
to him. Not even the leap of the youngest leopard
had ever delighted him so much.

'Here you see the bound man!' His very first movements drew a burst of applause which brought a flush
of excitement to the cheeks of the animal trainer, who
was standing at the edge of the ring. The bound man
rose up. His own surprise was again and again that
of a quadruped rearing up. He knelt, stood, leapt
and turned cartwheels. The surprise of the spectators
was like that of watching a bird which stays on the
ground from choice and gets no further than prepar-
ing to take off. All who came, came to see the bound
man—his elementary exercises, his ridiculous steps
and leaps made the tightrope walkers superfluous.
His fame grew from place to place, but his movements
remained always the same, namely few and fundamentally very ordinary movements, which he had to
practise in the daytime over and over again in the
semi-darkness of the tent, in order to maintain the
ease and lightness in his bonds. By remaining entirely
within them, he got rid of them, and because they did
not enclose him, they inspired him and gave his leaps
some direction. Like the wing-beats of birds of passage, when they set off in the warmth of summer and
fly hesitantly in little circles about the sky. The
children in the neighbourhood played from now on
nothing but 'Bound Man'. They took it in turns to
tie each other up, and one day the circus people came
across a little girl in a ditch, trussed up to the neck
and nearly suffocated. They freed her, and on that
evening, after the performance, the bound man spoke

to the spectators. He explained briefly that bonds which allow no leaps are pointless. From then on he was the centre of attraction as a joker.

Grass, sun, tent pegs knocked into the ground and pulled out again, villages nearby. 'Here you can see the bound man!' The summer grew to its zenith and shone lower and lower over the fish ponds in the hollows, took delight at its image in the dark mirror there, it flew away low over the riverbeds and made the plain what it was. All who were mobile followed the bound man. Many wanted to see the cords close up. So the circus owner declared every evening after the performance that those who wanted to convince themselves that the knots were really knots and not bows, and that the cord was really cord and not rubber bands, were quite welcome to do so. Usually the bound man waited for the people outside the tent; he laughed sometimes and sometimes he looked quite serious as he stretched out his arms to them. Many took the opportunity to look into his face, others gravely felt the cord and tested the knots at wrist and ankles, asking about the ratio of the cord lengths to the length of his limbs. They asked the bound man how it had all happened, and he patiently gave them always the same answer: well, he had been bound and, when he woke up, he found too that he had been robbed. Perhaps they had not had time to tie the cord properly, he added, because it was too slack for anyone who was not supposed to be able to move, and for someone who was supposed to be able to move, it was too tight. Yes, but you do move, they all answered. And he answered, well, what else was he to do?

Before he lay down, the bound man always stayed

up for a little by the fire. And when the circus owner then asked him why he never thought up any better stories, the bound man answered that he had never thought up even these. And at this he blushed, preferring to remain in the shadow.

He differed from the others in that he did not remove the cords even after the performance. For this reason every movement of his was worth seeing, and the village people crept around the site for a long time, solely to watch in case he should get up after several hours from the fire and roll himself into his blanket. And he saw their shadows moving off when the sky grew light again.

The circus owner often discussed how one could perhaps loosen the cords after the evening performance and tighten them again on the next morning. He consulted the tightrope walkers, for they after all did not spend all night on the rope— but no one took the matter seriously.

So that the bound man's fame rested on the fact that he never took his cords off, that, even when he washed, he had to wash all his clothes at the same time, and when he wanted to wash his clothes, he had to wash himself as well, so that he had no choice but to jump into the river every day, just as he was, as soon as the sun rose. And he had to take care not to venture out too far, in case he should be swept away.

The circus owner knew that the bound man's helplessness would protect him from the envy of the others if the need arose. Perhaps he was intentionally giving them the pleasure of watching him, his clothes clinging to him with wet, groping his way back to the bank carefully from stone to stone. And when the circus manager's wife said that even the best clothes would not stand up for ever to washing like that (and the bound man's clothes were anything but the best), he replied curtly that it was not going to be for ever. Thus he was able to reassure objectors: it was only intended for the summer. But he felt like a gambler, for he was not really serious about this. He was in fact quite prepared to sacrifice his lions and his tight-rope walkers for the bound man.

He proved that one night during which they leapt over the fire. Later, he became convinced that it was not the longer and shorter days which had caused this, but the bound man, who lay as usual by the fire, and who stared over it at them. With that smile of which one could never be sure whether it was the glow of the fire alone on his face. As one indeed knew nothing about him at all, for his stories never reached any further back than the moment when he emerged from the wood.

But that evening two of the circus people seized him by the arms and the legs, carried him near to the fire, swung him to and fro, while on the other side two others spread out their arms as though in joke. Then they threw him over, but they did not throw him far enough. The two others retreated a little—in order, as they said later, to take the impact better. The bound man landed very near the edge of the fire and would have been burnt if the circus owner had not taken him up in his arms and dragged him out of the fire to save the cords, which would have been the first to suffer from the flames. He was just as sure that the attack had really been made against the cords. He dismissed at once all who had taken part.

A few days later the circus owner's wife was awakened by groping steps in the grass and managed to get out in time to catch the clown in his last turn. With him he had only a pair of scissors. When he was questioned he repeated continually that he had not had designs on the bound man's life. He had wanted only to cut the cords. He asked to be given another chance, but he too was dismissed.

The bound man was amused by these attempts; he could free himself whenever he liked, but perhaps he still wanted to learn a few more new leaps. 'We have joined the circus, we have joined the circus!' Sometimes, when he lay awake at night, he recalled these children's rhymes. From the opposite bank of the river he could hear still the voices of the spectators, who had on their way home been driven too far downstream by the current. He saw the brightness of the river and the branches of the young trees under the moon, branches growing out of the dense willows; he still had no thought of autumn.

The circus owner dreaded the danger which sleep meant for the bound man. Not so much because there were always so many who aimed at freeing him— dismissed tightrope walkers or children who had been incited to stir up trouble—he could take action against them. The bound man himself was the greater danger, while asleep, he forgot the cords and was surprised by them on dark mornings. Angrily he tried to stand erect, reared up and fell back again. The jubilation of the previous evening had grown stale, sleep was still too near and his head and neck too free. He was the opposite of a hanged man, he had cords all round him everywhere but round his neck. Great care had at such times to be taken to ensure that he had no knife near him. The circus owner sometimes sent his wife to him towards morning. Whenever she found him asleep she tested the knots of the cord, which had become hard from dust and damp. She estimated the distance and touched his sore joints.

Soon there grew up the strangest rumours about the bound man. According to some he had bound himself and then invented the story about being robbed, and this opinion gained ground towards end of summer. Another, rather milder variation had it that he had had himself bound at his own request, it could even be that everything had happened as the result of a deal with the circus owner. The bound man's own halting narrative, his manner of suddenly breaking off whenever the conversation turned to the question of the attack, did much to give credit to these rumours. Anyone who now still believed the story of the thieves was laughed at. Nobody knew how difficult it was for the circus owner to keep the bound man, who declared often that he had had enough and wanted to go, so much of the summer had already been wasted.

Later on he never spoke about it any more. When the woman brought him his meals by the river and asked him how long he intended to go along with them, he gave no answer. She thought that, although he may not have got used to the cords, he certainly had never for a moment forgotten them—the only familarity the cords permitted. She asked him if he did not find it ridiculous to stay bound, but he answered no, it did not seem to him in the slightest ridiculous. So many creatures moved around with the circus, elephants, tigers, clowns, why should not a bound man go around with it as well? He told her also about his exercises, of new movements which he had learnt, about a move he had learnt while brushing

the flies away from the animals' eyes. He described
to her how he always forestalled the cords, how he
drew in his limbs just the smallest amount in order
not to stretch the cord, and she knew that there were
days when he hardly even touched them, when he
jumped down from the caravan and patted the sides
of the horses as though he were moving in a trance.
She watched him swing himself over the shafts,
touching the wood lightly as he did so, and she saw
the sun on his face. Sometimes, he told her, he felt
as if he were not bound at all. She answered that he
must never feel bound, if only he were ready to take
off the cord. Whereupon he said he was free to do
that at any time.

In the end she no longer knew whom she was most
worried about, the bound man or his cords. Although
she assured him that he could continue to go along
with them even were he not bound, she did not really
believe this. For what would his leaps and jumps
mean without his cords, what would he himself
mean without them? If they were removed, he would
just go and there would be an end to all the applause.
She would never again be able to sit beside him on
the stones, without rousing suspicion in the others,
and she knew that his closeness depended on the
cords, the bright evenings and the conversations, all
these things were centred only around the cords. As
soon as she understood the advantages of the cords,
he began to talk of the burden they were, and when
he spoke of the joy they brought she urged him to
take them off. It all seemed often as endless as the
summer itself.

At other times it alarmed her that her very words
seemed to hasten this end. There were times when

she jumped out of bed at night and ran across the grass to the place where the bound man lay asleep. She was about to shake him awake and to implore him to keep the cords on, but then she saw him lying in them like a dead man, the blanket thrown back, and his legs stretched out and his arms only slightly spread out. His clothes had suffered damage from the heat and the wet, but the cord had not become any thinner. And again it seemed to her certain that he would continue to move around with the circus until the skin fell away from his flesh and his limbs lay bared. On the next morning she would then urge him even more eagerly to take the cords off.

She placed her hope in the increasing cold. Autumn came and he would not be able much longer to jump into the water with his clothes on. But if he had hitherto been imperturbable, the thought towards the end of the summer that he might lose the cords plunged him into sadness. The songs of the harvesters filled him with fear : 'The summer, alas, is over.' But he did admit that he had to change his clothes. He refused to believe that one could do up the cord again, once it had been undone. About this time the circus owner talked of the idea of moving southwards this year.

Abruptly the heat changed into a dry, silent cold and the fires were kept burning all day. The bound man felt, as soon as he left the caravan, the cold grass under his feet. The tops of the grass blades were touched with frost. The horses stood dreamily and the beasts of prey seemed crouched ready to spring, even when asleep, to be gathering sadness under their skin ready for an outbreak.

On one of these days there escaped one of the

circus owner's young wolves. In order not to cause alarm he refrained from reporting it, but the wolf began to raid the cattle pastures in the neighbourhood. Although it was at first thought that it had been driven from far away by the foreboding of a hard winter, suspicion against the circus grew steadily. The circus owner was forced to take his employees into his confidence, and soon it could no longer be kept a secret where the wolf had come from. The circus people offered the local burgomasters their help in the hunt for the animal, but all hunting was in vain. Finally, the circus was quite openly accused of causing damage and general danger, and attendance figures fell.

The movements of the bound man had lost nothing of their stupefying ease when performed before the half-empty stands. During the daytime he wandered around on the nearby range of hills under the beaten silver of the autumn sky; as often as he could, he lay where the sun shone the longest. He also found a place which the dusk reached last, and he rose only unwillingly from the dry grass when it did at last reach him. When coming down again from the summit of the range of hills, he had to pass the copse on its southern slope, and on one of these evenings he saw two green lights gleaming up at him from below. He knew that they were not church windows and he was not deceived for a moment.

He stopped. The animal came up to him through thin vegetation. He was able now to distinguish its outline, the neck held at a sloping angle and the tail trailing on the ground, the lowered head. If he had not been bound, he would perhaps have been tempted to take to his heels, but as he was he felt not the slightest fear. He stood there calmly, his arms hang-

ing down and looked down at the bristling coat of
the animal, under which the muscles played like his
own limbs within the cords. He thought he could feel
the evening wind between him and the wolf, when the
animal sprang at him. The man tried to obey his cords.

With the care he had long practised he seized the
wolf by the throat. Tenderness for an equal, for the
erect one in the crouching one, rose up in him. In
one movement, resembling the swoop of a bird of
prey—and he knew now with certainty that flying is
possible only within a certain kind of bondage—he
hurled himself on the animal and brought it down.
As though in a slight intoxication he felt that he had
lost the deadly superiority of free limbs which causes
man's subjection.

He had in this struggle now the freedom to adapt
every flexion of his limbs to the cords, the freedom of
panthers, wolves and wild blossoms, which sway in
the evening wind. He landed with his head leaning
downwards at an angle, grasped with his naked feet
the animal's paws and its head with his hands.

He could feel the softness of the withered leaves
stroking the back of his hand, could feel his grip reach
without effort its greatest force, unhindered anywhere by the cords.

When he stepped out of the wood, a light rain
began to pour down, obscuring the sun. The bound
man stood for a while under the last row of trees.
Far away, down below and on the other side of the
thin veil of mist, denser from time to time when the
wind blew in short gusts, he could see the circus
encampment and the river, the meadows and pastures,
and the places where the cattle had crossed to and

fro. The thought occurred to him that he might well, after all, join in the move to the south. He laughed softly. It was against all reason. His clothes would not sustain much longer the rubbing of the cords, even if he could expect it of his joints to stay overcrusted, seeing that they broke open and bled when he made certain movements.

The circus owner's wife advised her husband to report the death of the animal, without naming the bound man. Not even at the time of the greatest jubilation would they have thought him capable of such a deed, and now, in their bitterness and at a time when it was already getting cold at night, they would be even less likely to think him capable of it. They would in the end not only doubt that he had killed the wolf, they would much rather be inclined to doubt that the wolf, which had on the very same day attacked a group of children at play, had even been killed at all. The circus owner, who had several wolves, could easily hang a wolf skin on the fence and charge no admission, and was not to be deterred. He, for his part, thought that the very announcement of such a deed could perhaps bring back the glory of the summer.

The bound man was uncertain in his movements on that evening; during one of his leaps he stumbled and fell. Even while he was still trying to get up, he could hear whistles and catcalls above him, which were like the calls of the birds at dawn. And, as happened sometimes to him on waking during the past summer, he tried to get up quickly, stretched the cords too tight and fell backwards. He lay still for a while, trying to regain his calm and heard the noise rise to a crescendo. 'How did you kill the wolf, bound man?' 'Are you the same man?' If he had been one of them, he would not have believed it himself. He thought that they were entitled to be resentful: a circus at this time of year, a bound man, an escaped wolf, and now this. There were a few groups which turned against each other, but most of the spectators thought that it was all a bad joke. When the bound man finally got on to his feet, the commotion was so great that he could hardly distinguish the individual words.

He saw them all rise up around him, like withered leaves blown by whirling storms round and round in a hollow, whose centre was still calm. He thought of the golden twilight of the past few days and he was seized with bitterness towards this funereal light over everything, a light that had spread on so many nights, bitterness towards the golden decoration hung by the godly in earlier times on dark paintings, bitterness towards all this backsliding.

They demanded that he should repeat the battle with the wolf. The circus owner pleaded that such a performance was not in the usual repertoire of a circus, and added that he did not keep animals just to have them killed before the eyes of his public. But they had already stormed over the enclosure and were rushing towards the cages. His wife ran along stands to the tent exit, which she succeeded in reaching from the other side. She pushed the attendant aside, whom the crowd had forced to open the gates, but the spectators pulled her back, so that she could no longer slam the gate to.

'Aren't you the one who lay all through the summer with him by the river?' 'What's it like when he puts his arms round you?' She shouted to them that they need not believe him if they didn't want to, and that they had never really deserved to have and see a bound man, and that painted clowns were good enough for them.

To the bound man it seemed as if he had expected this outburst of laughter ever since early May; what had tasted so nice all summer was now stinking. But if they really wanted it, he would this very night take on all the circus animals. He had never yet felt so at one with the cords.

Gently he pushed aside the woman who barred his way. Good gracious, perhaps he would in spite of all go southwards with them. He stood at the open door, watching the animal rear up, a strong, young animal, and heard at the same time the circus owner behind him complaining about the lost wolves. He clapped his hands in order to attract the animal's attention, and, when it was near enough, he turned back in order to close the iron grille. He looked into the woman's face. Suddenly he remembered the circus owner's warning that he would accuse anyone whom he found with a sharp object anywhere near the bound man of murderous intentions. At the same time he felt the blade near his wrist, as cool as river water in autumn, which he had in the last few weeks hardly been able to face. The cord fell down on one side of him, and became entangled, when he tried to separate it from the other. He pushed the woman back, but his movements tended already to be aimless. Had he not been on the qui vive enough when faced with his would-be liberators, when faced with this pity which had tried to lull him into a sense of false security? Had he indeed lain too long beside the river? He wished she would have chosen to cut the cord in any other moment than this.

He was standing now inside the cage, while he tore the cords from him like the remains of a sloughed snake skin. It amused him a lot to see the spectators fall back all around him. Did they know that he had now no alternative? Or would a fight have proved anything at all now? At the same time he felt all his blood flowing downwards, and he suddenly felt weak.

The wolf was embittered by the cords, which seemed to him to be a snare, more by this than the fact that a stranger had entered his cage. He crouched, ready to spring. The man staggered over and grasped the weapon which hung on the wall of the cage. And then, before anyone could prevent him, he shot the animal between the eyes. The animal reared up and its body brushed him slightly as it fell.

On his way to the river he heard the steps of the pursuers behind him, the spectators, the tightrope walkers, the circus owner himself, and, slowest of all, those of the woman. He hid behind a clump of bushes and watched them all run past him and go back slowly after a time to the encampment. The moon shone on the meadows, and it had at this time the colour of growth and of death.

When he came to the river his anger had subsided. In the dawn light it seemed to him as if there were ice floes on the water, as if, over there, in the pastures there had already fallen snow, which removes all memory.

LIFE STORY IN RETROSPECT

When someone pushes your bed out of the ward, when you see that the sky is growing green and when

65

you want to save the priest the trouble of holding a funeral service, then it is time for you to get up, softly, as children do when in the mornings the light shines through the shutters, secretly, so that the nurse doesn't see—and quickly!

But the priest has already begun, you can hear his voice, young and eager and undeterred, you can already hear him speaking. Let it be! Let his kind words be submerged in the pouring rain. Your grave is open. Let his easy confidence first become helpless, so that it may receive help. If you let him go on he will in the end no longer know whether he has even begun. And because he doesn't know, he makes the usual sign to the pall-bearers. And the pall-bearers don't ask many questions, they just bring your coffin up again. And they take the wreath off the lid and give it back to the young man who stands at the side of the grave with bowed head. The young man takes his wreath and in his embarrassment smoothes the ribbons on it; for a moment he raises his head and the rain blows a few tears down his cheeks. Then the procession starts off back again along by the wall. The candles in the ugly little chapel are lit again and the priest reads the committal service, so that you can live. He shakes the young man's hand warmly and, out of sheer embarrassment, wishes him luck. It is the first time he has ever conducted a funeral service and he blushes to the roots of his hair. And before he can correct himself, the young man has disappeared. What still remains to be done? When someone has wished a mourner luck, there is nothing else to be done but send the dead home again.

Immediately afterwards the vehicle with your coffin drives slowly up the street again. To right and left are houses, and there are yellow narcissi in all the windows, the same ones that are woven into all the wreaths, and there is nothing to be done about it. Children press their faces to the closed windows, it is raining but one of them is certain to run out of the house. He clambers on to the back of the hearse but is pushed off and drops back. The child shields its eyes with both hands and gazes sullenly at you all. What else is one to swing up on if you live in the road that leads to the cemetery?

Your hearse waits at the cross roads for the green light. The rain has slackened. Rain-drops dance on the roof of the car. One can smell the hay from the distance. The streets have been freshly christened and the sky lays its hand on all the roofs. Out of sheer politeness your hearse drives for a little alongside the tram. Two little boys at the side of the road lay bets. But the one who bets on the tram will lose. You could have warned him, but no one has ever won a bet about a body rising from a coffin.

Be patient. For it is early summer. Mornings still reach back far into the night. You'll be all right. Before it is dark and all the children have gone from the side of the road, the car is already turning in to the hospital yard and a ray of moonlight falls at this moment across the entrance. The men come at once and lift your coffin from the hearse, which now drives off back home happily.

They carry your coffin through the second doorway across the yard into the morgue. There the empty pedestal stands waiting, black, sloping and high up, and they place the coffin on it and open it again; one of them swears because the nails have been knocked in too hard. Such damned efficiency!

67

Immediately afterwards the young man comes back bringing the wreath and none too soon. The men arrange the ribbons on it and lay the wreath at the front, you can rest assured that the wreath is in a good position. By tomorrow the faded flowers will have revived and will close up as if in bud. All night long you will be alone, the cross between your hands, and even in the daytime you will be at peace. Later you will never be able to manage to lie so still.

The next day the young man comes again. And because the rain drives no tears into his face, he stares blankly ahead, twiddling his cap in his hands. Only just before they lift the coffin on to the boards again does he cover his face with his hands, weeping. You are to stay no longer in the morgue. Why is he weeping? The lid of the coffin is just left on loosely and it is bright daylight. The sparrows chirrup happily. They do not know that it is forbidden to wake the dead. The young man walks ahead of your coffin as if there were glasses between his steps. The wind is cool and wayward, a petulant child.

They carry you into the house and up the stairs. You are lifted out of the coffin. Your bed has been freshly made. The young man stares through the window down into the yard where two cooing pigeons are copulating; disgusted, he turns away.

And by now they have put you back into bed. And they have bound the cloth under your chin again, the cloth that makes you look so strange. The man begins to wail, throwing himself across you. They lead him gently away. 'Quiet, please' notices are on all the walls, the hospitals are at this time over-crowded, the dead must not awake too soon.

Over in the harbour the ships are hooting. Does it

mean arrival or departure? Who can know that?
Silence! Quiet please! Do not awake the dead before
it is time, for they sleep lightly. But the ships go on
hooting. And a little later they will have to take the
cloth from your chin again, whether they want to
or not. And they will wash you and change your
linen, and one of them will lean over your heart,
quickly, while you are still dead. There is not much
more time, and that is the ships' fault. It is getting
darker outside. They open your eyes, which shine
white. They no longer talk about how peaceful you
look, thank heavens for that, the words die away in
their mouths. But wait! They will soon have gone.
No one wants to be a witness, for people are still
burnt for that.

They leave you alone. They leave you so alone that
you open your eyes and see the green sky, they leave
you so alone that you begin to breathe, heavily,
gaspingly and deeply, rattling like an anchor chain
running out. You rear up and cry out for your
mother. How green the sky is! 'The feverishness is
passing off and the death agony is beginning,' says a
voice behind you.

Oh, they! What do they know?

Go now! Now is the moment. All have been called
away. Go, before they come back and before their
loud whispering starts again, go down the stairs, past
the porter, out through the morning which turns to
night. The birds cry in the darkness, as if your pains
had begun to rejoice. Go home! Go and lie down in
your own bed again, even if the frame does creak
and even if it is unmade still. You will get better
quicker there! There you will rage and storm against
your own self for three days only, and will drink your

fill of the green sky, for three days only you will push aside the soup which the woman from upstairs brings you, and on the fourth you will eat it.

And on the seventh, which is the day of rest, on the seventh, you will go away. You are pursued by pain, but you will find the way. To the left first and right, and then to the left again, across the streets near the harbour which are so wretched that they can do nothing else than lead to the sea. If only the young man were near you, but the young man is not with you, you were much more beautiful in your coffin. But now your face is distorted with pain, the pain which has ceased to rejoice. And now the sweat has broken out on your forehead again, all the way along; no, in your coffin you were much more beautiful!

The children are playing ball in the roadway. You run into them, you run as if going backwards and none of them is your child. How could one of them be your child, if you go to the old woman who lives near the pub? The whole harbour knows how she pays for all the gin she drinks.

She is already waiting at the door. The door is open and she stretches out her dirty hand towards you. Everything there is dirty. On the chimney piece stand the yellow flowers, and they are the same ones which they weave into wreaths, they are the same ones. And the old woman is far too friendly. And here too the stairs creak. And the steamers hoot, it does not matter where you go, they are always hooting. And you are shaken by pain, but you must not cry out. The steamers hoot but you must not cry out. The steamers can hoot but you must not cry out. Give the old woman the money for gin! Once you have given her the money she keeps your mouth shut with both hands. She is quite sober from gin, the old woman. She does not dream of the unborn children. The innocent children do not dare to complain to the saints about her, nor do the guilty ones. But— you do! 'Bring my child back to life again!'

No one has ever made a request like that to the old woman. But you do. The mirror gives you strength. The blank, fly-blown mirror makes you demand what no one else has ever demanded.

'Bring it back to life or I will knock your yellow flowers over, or I will scratch your eyes out, or I will throw open the windows of your place and shout across the street, so that they will all be able to hear what they already know, I will shout. . . .'

At that the old woman becomes frightened, and in her great fear, in the blank mirror, she grants your request. She does not know what she is doing, but in the blank mirror she manages it. Fear becomes intense and the pain becomes raging again. And before you cry out you know the lullaby: 'Sleep, baby, sleep'. And before you cry out, the mirror hurls you down the dark stairs again and lets you go, lets you get away. Do not run too fast!

It is better to look up from the ground, otherwise it could happen that you run into a young man down there amongst the planks lying around at the empty building site, into a young man twiddling his cap in his hands. That is how you recognise him. He is the same one who stood beside your coffin, twiddling his cap, there he is again! Standing here as though he had never been away, leaning there against the planks. You fall into his arms. He has no tears any more, so give him some of yours. And say good-bye before you link arms with him. Say good-bye! You will never forget even if he does: one says farewell right at the beginning. Before you go off together you must part for ever by the planks around the empty building site.

And then you both go on further. There is a road which leads past the coal dumps to the sea. You are both silent. You are waiting for the first word and are leaving it to him, so that it is not you who will have to end the matter. What will he say? Quickly, before you both reach the sea which brings such uncertainy! What is he saying? What is his first word? Can it really be so difficult that it makes him stutter and forces him to look down at the ground? Or is it the heaps of coal, looming up behind the planks, casting shadows under his eyes and dazzling him with their blackness? The first word—now he has said it: it is the name of a back street. It is the one in which the old woman lives. Is it really possible? Even before he knows that you are expecting the child, he already tells you the name of the old woman; even before he says he loves you, he tells you about the old woman. Say nothing yet! He does not know that you already were at the old woman's; he can't know, he knows nothing about the mirror. But he has hardly spoken the words, when he has forgotten them. In the mirror one says everything, in order that it may be forgotten. And you have hardly said that you are expecting the child, when you concealed the fact. The mirror tells everything. The coal heaps fade away behind you, you have both reached the sea and can see the white boats like questions at the limit of your view, be silent, both of you, the sea takes the answer from your mouth, the sea swallows up what you were about to say. From then on you both walk many times along the beach, as though you were going down along it homewards, as though you were running away, away, as though you were going home.

What are they whispering in their light-coloured bonnets? 'That is the death agony.' Oh, let them talk.

One day the sky will be pale enough, so pale that its paleness will shine.

On this day the blank mirror reflects the condemned house. People say a house is condemned when it is going to be pulled down; condemned, they say, they don't know any better. Neither of you need be afraid. The sky is now pale enough. And, like the sky in its paleness, the house too at the end of its condemnation awaits ecstasy. Tears come easily from much laughter. You have cried enough. Take back your wreath. Soon now you will be able also to loosen your plaits. It is all in the mirror. And behind all that you do the sea lies green. It lies before you when you leave the house. When you climb out again through the caving windows you have already forgotten. In the mirror everything is done that it might be forgiven.

And from then on he urges you to go in with him. But in your eagerness you both withdraw from it and turn away from the beach. You do not turn round. And the condemned house stands there behind you. You go up along the river, and your own feverishness flows up and past you both. Soon his insistence slackens. And at the same moment you are no more willing, and you both become shyer. That is the tide flowing out, drawing the sea away from all coasts. Even river levels are lower at ebb tide. And over there on the other side the tree-crowns finally emerge beyond the tops of lesser trees. Below them the shingle roofs slumber.

Take care, he will soon begin to talk about the future, of many children and of a long life, his cheeks burning with eagerness as he does so. Even yours are lit by it. You will both argue about whether you want sons and daughters, and you would rather have sons. And he would prefer a tiled roof, and you want ——— but by now you have already gone far too far up the river. You are seized with fear. The shingle roofs on the other side are out of sight, and there are there now only fields and damp meadows. And here? You should both watch out for the road. It is growing dusk —as soberly as it does only in the mornings. The future is all over. The future is a pathway beside the river, which flows into the meadows. Go back, both of you.

And now what is to happen?

Three days later he no longer dares to put his arm round your shoulder. And three days after that he asks you what your name is, and you ask him his. And now neither of you even knows the other's name. And you don't even ask any more. It is better like that.

And now at last you both walk silently side by side once more. And if he asks you anything now, it is only to ask if it is going to rain. Who can tell? You become more and more estranged from each other. You have long ago given up talking to each other about the future. You no longer meet very often, but you are still not estranged enough. Wait a while, be patient. One day this stage too will have been reached. One day he will be so strange to you that you will begin to love him in an open doorway in some back street. All in its own good time. Now it has come.

'It won't last much longer,' they are saying behind you, 'it's nearly over!'

What do they know? Isn't it just the beginning?

A day will come when you will see him for the first time. And he you. For the first time means: never again. But don't be afraid. There is no need for you to say farewell to each other, you did that long ago. How good that you have already done so!

It will be an autumn day, a day full of expectation that all the fruits around us will one day become flowers, an autumn day like this, with this light-coloured smoke and with shadows which lie like splinters between one's steps, ones you could cut your feet on, the sort you could stumble over when you're sent for apples in the market, you could fall over through sheer hope and happiness. A young man comes to your aid. His jacket is thrown only lightly over his shoulders and he smiles, twiddling his cap in his hands, and is tongue-tied. But you are both happy in this last light. You thank him, throwing your head back a little, your plaits loosen and fall down. 'Oh,' he says, 'aren't you still going to school?' He turns and goes off whistling. And you part like this, without looking at each other again even once, entirely without any grief and without even knowing that you are parting.

Now you can play with your little brothers again, and you can go along by the river with them, the pathway by the river under the alders, and over there are the white shingle roofs as usual amongst the tree-tops. What will the future bring? Certainly no sons. But it has brought you brothers, plaits, making them

75

dance and blush and laugh behind their hands. But wait only a year and you will be able to jump over the rope and snatch at the branches hanging over the walls. You have already learnt foreign languages but it is not so easy. Your own language is much harder. It is even harder to learn to read and write, but it is hardest to forget everything. And if you had to know everything at the first examination, then you may at the end be allowed to know nothing. Will you pass? Will you sit still enough? If you are afraid enough not to open your mouth, all will be well.

You hang again for ever on its hook the blue cap which all schoolchildren wear, and you leave school. It is autumn again. The flowers have long since budded again, the buds have withered away again to fruit. Everywhere the little children are going home, they have passed their examination, like you. But none of you know anything any more. You are on your way home, your father is waiting for you, and your little brothers are crying as loud as they can and pull your hair. You quieten them and comfort your father.

Soon the summer comes, with its long days. Soon your mother dies. You and your father, you both fetch her from the cemetery. For three days she lies surrounded by crackling candles, as you did that time. Blow out the candles, before she wakes up! But she already smells the wax and raises herself up on her arms and complains softly about the waste. Then she gets up and changes her clothes.

It is as well that your mother dies, for you could not have managed alone with your little brothers much longer. But now she is there. Now she attends to everything, and teaches you to play much better, one can never learn to do it well enough. And it is not an easy thing to do. But it is still not the most difficult thing.

The most difficult thing is to forget how to speak and how to walk, and instead to stammer and to crawl on the floor, only in the end to be wrapped in nappies. The most difficult thing is to endure tenderness and affectionate attention and just to gaze in front of one. Be patient! Soon all will be well. God will know the day, on which you will be weak enough.

And that is the day of your birth. You come into the world and open your eyes and shut them again in the strong light. The light warms your limbs, you move in the sun, you have arrived, you are alive. Your father bends down over you.

Behind you they are saying: 'It is all over, she is dead!'

Hush! let them talk!

LAKE SPIRITS

Throughout the summer one pays little heed to them or one treats them as one's equals, and those who leave the lake when summer goes will never recognise them. Only towards autumn do they begin to stand out more clearly. Anyone who comes later or who stays longer, anyone who himself no longer knows if he is one of the guests or the ghosts, will be able to distinguish them. For just in early autumn there are days when outlines at moments of change become once again very clear.

There is the man, who, just before landing, could not stop the engine of his boat. He thought at first that this was no great misfortune, and fortunately the lake was big, turned round and drove from the east bank back to the west bank, where the mountains rise up steeply and where the big hotels are. It was a fine evening, and his children waved to him from the landing stage, but he still could not stop his engine, pretended that he did not want to land, and drove back again to the flat bank. Here— amongst distant sailing boats, lake shore and swans, who had ventured far out—at the sight of the red glow cast by the setting sun on the eastern shore, he broke out in perspiration for the first time, because he still could not stop his engine. He called cheerfully to his friends sitting drinking coffee on the hotel terrace that he wanted to drive round a little longer, and they called back cheerfully, encouraging him to do so. When he came by for the third time he called out that he just wanted to fetch his children, and to his children he called out that he was going to fetch his friends. Soon after this friends and children had disappeared from both shores, and when he came by a fourth time, he called out no more.

He had discovered that his petrol tank was leaky, the petrol had long since run out, but his engine ran on lake water. He no longer thought that this was a misfortune, fortunately the lake was big. The last steamer came past and the people shouted in high spirits to him, but he did not answer, he only thought: 'What if no more boats come past?' And soon no more did come past. The yachts lay with furled sails in the bays and the hotels were reflected in the water of the lake. Thick mist began to rise, the man drove in all directions, and then along the shore, somewhere a girl was still swimming, plunging into the wake of his boat, and then she too went on land.

But, while driving, he could not plug the leak in his petrol tank, and so he just drove on and on. Now he was only consoled by the thought that his tank would one day have sucked up all the water in the lake, and he reflected that it was a strange way to sink, just to suck up all the water in a lake and end up on the dry bottom. Soon after this it began to rain, so that thought did not comfort him any more. When he next came past the house, outside which the girl had been bathing, he saw that there was still light behind one of the windows, but, further up shore, in the windows behind which his children were sleeping, it was already dark, and when he shortly afterwards drove back again, the girl too had extinguished her light. The rain had stopped, but that afforded him no comfort any more.

On the next morning his friends, breakfasting on the terrace, were surprised to see him on the water so early. He called out cheerfully to them, saying that the summer was drawing to a close and that one must take advantage of every minute, and he said the same to his children, standing early on the landing stage. And when, on the following morning, they wanted to send out a rescue party to fetch him in, he waved them away, for he could now, having pretended cheerfulness for two days, hardly admit the necessity of a rescue party, especially not in the eyes of the girl, who daily awaited the wake of his boat in the evening. On the fourth day he began to be afraid that they might be making fun of him, but he drew comfort from the fact that this too would pass. And it did.

With the cooler weather his friends left, and his children too returned to the town and school began. Sounds of motors on the lake shore became less and less, and his boat on the water was the only sound left. The mist hanging over the woods on the hillside became increasingly thicker, and the smoke from the chimneys hung still in the tree tops.

The girl was the last to leave the lake. From the water he could see her loading her cases into the car. She blew him a kiss and thought: 'If he were some haunted spirit, I would have stayed here longer, but he is only a sensual pleasure seeker!'

Soon afterwards, out of sheer despair, he ran his boat at this spot up onto the gravel beach. The boat was ripped open lengthways and drives now on air. In the autumn nights the locals can hear it roaring past over their heads.

Or the woman who disintegrates as soon as she takes her sunglasses off.

This was not always so. There were times when she played in the sand in bright sunshine; then she did not wear sunglasses. And there were also times when she put on sunglasses as soon as the sun shone in her face, and she took them off again as soon as the sun went in—and yet she did not disintegrate. But is long ago, and if you were to ask her how long ago it was, she would not be able to tell you, and she would not even tolerate such a question.

This unfortunate state of affairs probably started on that day when she began not to take her sunglasses off even in the shade, during that car ride in the spring when it suddenly became overcast and everybody except her took off their sunglasses. But one should never wear sunglasses in the shade; they will make you pay for it.

When, a little after this, during a trip on a friend's yacht, she took her sunglasses off for a moment, she felt herself suddenly turning into nothing, her arms and legs dissolved in the east wind. And this east wind, which drives the little white horses on the waves of the lake, would have as sure as anything whisked her overboard, if she had not had the presence of mind to put her sunglasses on again at once. The same east wind fortunately brought good weather, sun and great heat, and so, for the next few weeks, she attracted no further attention. When dancing in the evenings she explained to anyone who asked her that she wore the sunglasses against the strong light of the arc lamps, and soon many began to imitate her. Admittedly nobody knew that she wore her sunglasses also at night, for she slept with her bedroom window open and had no desire to be swept out of the room or to wake up next morning and find that she just wasn't there.

When, for a short time, dull, rainy weather set in, she tried once again to take her sunglasses off, but fell immediately into the same state of dissolution as the first time, and realised that the west wind too was prepared to carry her off. And so she never tried again after that, but kept aloof for a time, waiting for the sun to come again. And the sun did come again, again and again all through the summer. And then she sailed on her friends' yachts, played tennis or went swimming, with her sunglasses on all the time, out into the lake. And she kissed this or that fellow and did not even take her sunglasses off for that. She discovered that one can do almost anything in the world with sunglasses on. As long as it was summer.

But now autumn is gradually coming. Most of her friends have gone back to town, and only a few have remained. And she herself—what could she do with sunglasses in the town? Here they all treat her whim as a personal gimmick, and as long as there are sunny days and the last of her friends are still around her, nothing will change. But the wind blows more fiercely every day, friends and sunny days are getting fewer. And there is no question that she could ever take her sunglasses off again.

What will happen when winter comes?

And there were those three girls, standing in the stern of the steamer and poking fun at the only sailor on the steamer. They went on board at the flat shore, rode over to the hilly shore to have coffee and then went back again to the flat shore.

From the very first moment the sailor noticed them laughing behind their hands and calling out things which he could not understand, because of the noise made by the steamer. But he had the definite suspicion that it concerned him and the steamer; and when he climbed down from his place beside the captain to check the tickets and thus came near to the girls, their amusement increased so much that he felt his suspicions confirmed. He snarled at them, asking to see their tickets, but they had already bought them, so that all he could do was mark them. While he was doing this one of the girls asked him if he had no other occupation than this in winter, and he answered: 'No.' And they began to laugh again.

But from that moment he had the feeling that his cap-badge was missing, and he found it hard to check the rest of the tickets. He climbed back up to the captain, but this time he did not take the children of the day-trippers up with him as usual. And he could see the lake down there below him, calm and green, and he could see the sharp bow of the steamer cutting into the water—an ocean steamer could not have cut into the water any sharper—but today even that did not bring him any peace. Rather was he irritated by the notice 'Mind your head!' which was fixed above the door to the cabins, and by the black smoke which blew down from the funnel to the stern, blackening the fluttering flag, as if he were to blame for it.

No, he did nothing else in winter. Well, why does the steamer ply in winter, they asked him, when he came past them again. 'Mails!' he said. In a clear moment he saw them talking quietly together, and that comforted him for a while; but when the steamer tied up and he threw the rope over the bollard on the little jetty, they began to laugh again, although he had hit the bollard with the loop of the rope exactly, and as long as he watched them he was still ill at ease.

One hour later they came on board again, but the sky had in the meantime grown overcast, and when they were in the middle of the lake, the thunderstorm broke out. The boat began to rock and the sailor seized the opportunity to show the girls what he was worth. In his oilskin he climbed more often than was necessary over the railing, round on the outside and back again. In doing so, he slipped on the wet wood, since it had begun to rain even harder, and fell into the lake. And beacuse he had one thing in common with sailors on ocean steamers, namely that he could not swim, and because the lake had that in common with the open sea, namely that one can drown in it, he drowned.

He rests in peace, as it says on his gravestone, for they fetched him out. But the three girls still travel on the steamer and stand in the stern and laugh behind their hands. Anyone who sees them should not be put off by them. They are always the same.

WHERE I LIVE

Since yesterday I have been living one storey lower. I don't want to say it out loud, but I am living lower down. I don't want to say it out loud because I have not properly moved in. I came back last night from the concert, as usual on Saturday evening, and, after unlocking the main door, and pressing the light switch, I went upstairs. I went upstairs without any misgivings—the lift has been out of order since the war—and when I had reached the third floor I thought : 'I wish I were already home' and leaned for a moment against the wall by the door of the lift. On the third floor I am usually overcome by a kind of exhaustion, which sometimes is so excessive that I feel as though I had already gone up four flights of stairs. But I did not think that this time, I knew that I had one more floor above me. So I opened my eyes again, in order to go up the last flight, when I caught sight of my name-plate on the door beside the lift. Had I made a mistake and gone after all up four flights of stairs? I was about to look at the name board, indicating the flat occupants, but just at that moment the light went out.

As the light switch is on the other side of the hall-way, I walked the two steps to my door in the dark and unlocked it. To my door, did I say? Well, what other door could it be, if it had my name on it? I *must* have gone up four flights of stairs.

The door opened without any effort, I found the switch and stood in the bright hall, in my own hall, where everything was as usual : the red wallpaper, which I had intended long ago to change, the seat set against it, and, on the left, the corridor leading to the kitchen. Everything was as usual. In the kitchen lay the bread I had left over from supper, still in the bread bin. All was unchanged. I cut off a slice of bread and began to eat, then I remembered suddenly that I had not yet shut the door into the hallway when I came in, and went back through my own hall to close it.

While doing so I noticed, in the light which shone out from my hall into the staircase outside, the board with the names of the flat occupants on it. There it stood quite plainly : 'Third Floor.' I ran out, pressed the light switch and read it again. Then I read the name plates on the other doors. They were all names of people who had previously lived below me. I thought for a moment of going up the stairs to make sure which people were now living next to those who used to live next to me, whether, for example, the doctor who had previously lived below me, now in fact lived above me; but I suddenly felt so tired and worn out that I just had to go to bed.

I've been lying awake ever since, wondering what's going to happen tomorrow. From time to time I feel tempted to get up and to go upstairs and to try to make certain. But I feel too weak, and perhaps some-one up there could be awakened by the light in the stairway and could come out and ask me : 'What do you want here?' And I am so afraid of a question like this from one of my former neighbours that I prefer to lie awake, although I know that it will be even more difficult to go upstairs in daytime.

In the next room I can hear the breathing of the student who is my lodger; he is a student of marine engineering and breathes deeply and evenly. He has no idea of all this that has happened. He has no idea, and here I lie awake. I wonder if I ought to ask him tomorrow. He does not go out very often and most likely he was at home while I was at the concert. He ought to know really. Perhaps I should ask the cleaner as well.

No, I won't. How could I ask anyone who does not ask me? How could I go up to him and say : 'I wonder if you know if I lived one floor higher yesterday?' And what could he say to that? My only hope is that someone will ask me, ask me tomorrow : 'Excuse me, but didn't you live one storey higher yesterday?' But I know my cleaner woman well enough to know that she won't ask me anything. Or perhaps one of my former neighbours : 'Surely you were living next to us yesterday, weren't you?' Or perhaps it might be one of my new neighbours. But I know them all well enough to be sure that none of them will ask anything. So then the only thing left for me will be to pretend that I have lived all my life a floor lower.

I wonder, too, what would have happened if I had left the concert before it had ended. But from today onwards, this question is just as pointless as all other questions. I will try to get to sleep.

I am living now in the cellar. It has at least the advantage that my cleaner woman hasn't got to go all the way down to get the coal, because we keep it in the next room, and she seems to be quite satisfied with the arrangement. I suspect that she asks no questions because it is so much more convenient for for her like this. She never was very keen on tidying up; least of all here. It would be ridiculous to expect her to wipe the coal dust off the furniture every hour. Looking at her I can see that she is quite content. And the student runs up the steps every day whistling and comes back again in the evening. I can hear him breathing deeply and regularly at night. I sometimes wish he would bring a girl home one evening, who would be surprised to find him living in a cellar; but he never does bring a girl home with him.

And nobody else asks. The coalmen who unload their sacks in the cellars to right and left with a lot of noise, doff their caps with a greeting, when I encounter them on the stairs. Quite often they even put their coal sacks down and stand and wait till I have passed. The caretaker, too, greets me civilly, when he sees me before I go out at the door. I thought for a moment that his greeting was a little more friendly than usual, but it was only my imagination. Quite a lot seems friendly to one emerging from a cellar.

In the street I stop and wipe the coal dust off my coat, but only a little sticks to it. It is my winter coat, a dark one. I am surprised in the tram that the conductor treats me like the other passengers and that no one edges away from me. I wonder what things will be like when I live in the canal. For I am slowly getting used to this idea.

Since I have been living in the cellar, I still go occasionally to the concert. Mostly Saturdays, but also sometimes in the middle of the week. After all, I could not prevent myself from going, just because one day I landed up in the cellar. I am now often surprised at my self-reproaches at all the things which I connected in the beginning with this descent into the cellar. At first I just kept thinking : 'If only I had not gone to the concert or across the road for a glass of wine!' But I don't think like that any more. Since I have come to live in the cellar, I feel much calmer, and go across the road for a glass of wine as often as I feel like it. It would be useless to be anxious about the vapours in the canal, for I ought then to be anxious about the fires in the earth's interior— there are so many things which I ought to be anxious about. And even if I were to stay at home all the time and never even go out into the street, I would still end up one day in the canal.

I wonder only what my cleaner woman would say to that. She would certainly be freed from the necessity of airing the place. And the student would go whistling up through the canal hatches and come down through them again. I wonder too about the concert and the glass of wine then. And what if the student got the idea just at that very time to bring a girl home with him? I wonder if my rooms would be the same, even in the canal. They have been, up till now, but in the canal there is no house any more. And I can't imagine that the division into rooms and kitchen and drawing-room and student's room would be the same in the interior of the earth.

But, up till now, nothing has changed. The red wallpaper, and the chest standing in front of it, the little corridor down to the kitchen, every picture on the wall, the old armchairs and the bookshelves—even every single book in them. The bread bin out there and the curtains at the windows.

Ah, the windows, the windows have changed. But at that time I was mostly in the kitchen, and from time immemorial the kitchen window has looked out on to the hallway. It was always barred. So I have no reason to go to the caretaker for that, even less because of the view. He could quite rightly say that a view is no part of a flat; the rent is charged according to the size, not according to the view. He could perfectly well tell me that the view is my own affair.

And I shan't go to him, I am quite content as long as he is agreeable. The only thing I could complain about might perhaps be that the windows are half as small as they were. But, here again, he could well answer that there is no other possibility in a cellar. And what could I say to that? I couldn't say that I am not used to this because I used to live on the fourth floor. In such a case I ought to have complained while I was still on the third floor. But it is too late now.

MY GREEN DONKEY

Every day I see a green donkey walking across the railway bridge, his hooves clattering over the planks and his head showing up over the railing. I don't know where he comes from, I have not been able to observe that. But I suspect he comes from the abandoned electricity works on the other side of the bridge, from where the road leads in a straight line to the north-west (a direction I have never had much time for anyhow) and in whose tumble-down entrance soldiers stand in the evenings cuddling their girls as soon as it is dark and only a feeble shred of light lies on the rusty roof. But my donkey comes earlier. He doesn't come at midday, for example, or shortly after, when the sun beats down glaringly on every one of the deserted farms over there, penetrating even the cracks of the nailed-up windows. No, he comes at the first almost imperceptible fading of the light; it is then that I see him, mostly already up there on the bridge or climbing the steps up to it. I have only once seen him when he had already reached the other side of the railway line, trotting along the paving stones, but he looked then as if he were in a hurry, as though he were late. I thought then that I had seen him coming out of the half-open door of the electricity works, which stood there silent in the heat.

He takes no notice whatever of railway employees or of any other people who go across the bridge; he just politely makes way for them, and even the occasional trains which pass under the bridge, roaring and whistling, while he trots by overhead, leave him quite indifferent. Often he turns his head sideways and looks down, mostly when no train is passing, and not for very long. It seems to me then that he may be exchanging a few words with the railway lines, but I suppose that is hardly possible. And why should he? Once he has passed midway over the bridge, he disappears, after some hesitation and without turning back. There is one thing I *am* certain about and that is the manner in which he disappears. I can understand that quite well, for why should he take all the trouble to turn back, since he knows the way so well?

But how does he come, where does he come from, where does he originate from? Has he a mother or a bed of hay in one of the silent farms over there? Or does he live in one of the former offices where he has his own corner or piece of wall? Or is his origin like that of the lightning, in the former pylons and trailing power cables? I admit I do not know just how the lightning originates, and I don't want to know, apart from the fact that my donkey might have the same sort of origin. *My* donkey? That is saying a lot. But I will not take back what I said. Certainly it is possible that others see him too, but I won't ask them. My donkey, whom I neither feed nor water, whose coat I don't rub down and whom I don't comfort. But his shape is outlined against the background of the distant range of hills so clearly like the hills themselves against the afternoon. So, in my eyes, *my* donkey. Why should I not confess that I live for the moment when he comes? That his appearance makes me catch my breath, none but he, his shape, the different shades of green on him, and his way of lowering his head and looking down at the railway lines? I thought he might perhaps be hungry and be on the look-out for the grass and sparse weeds growing between the railway sleepers. But one must control one's sympathy. I am old enough for that and I won't be laying a bundle of hay for him on the bridge. He doesn't look bad or hungry or ill-treated—nor does he look particularly good. But there are surely few donkeys that look particularly good. I don't want to make the old mistake and demand too much of him. I will be content with merely expecting him, or, rather : with not expecting him. For he doesn't come regularly. Did I forget to say that? Twice he hasn't come. I write this hesitatingly, for perhaps this is the rhythm he is used to, perhaps there is for him no twice, and he came regularly, he came always, and would be surprised at this complaint. As he seems to be surprised over many things. Surprise, yes, that is what characterises him best, what distinguishes him, I think. I am determined to confine myself to suppositions as far as he is concerned, and later on to even fewer. But, until then, there is much that disturbs me. More, for example, than the fact that he might possibly be hungry, that I don't know where he sleeps, where he rests, where he was born perhaps. For he does need rest. It could be that he needs death even each time, I don't know. I consider it very exhausting to walk as green as he does over the bridge every evening, to gaze round as he does and then to disappear.

A donkey like this needs rest, a lot of rest. I wonder if a disused electricity works is the right place for that, whether it is sufficient? I wonder if the trailing cables stroke him softly enough, once he has left here, in the night he spends? For his night is longer than ours. And I wonder too if the outline of the hills show him enough friendship during the day he has to spend. For his day is shorter. As usual I don't know. And I shall never find out, for my aim can be none other than to know less and less of him, this much have I learnt in the six months or so that he has been coming. Learnt from him. And so I shall probably learn to accept the fact that the day will come when he will appear no more; I fear this will be so. Perhaps he could stay away when the cold weather comes, and that might perhaps be as much a part of his coming as the coming itself. And until then I am determined to learn so little of him that I shall be able to endure his failure to come, that I then direct my gaze no longer at the bridge.

But, until I reach that stage, I often dream that he might possibly have a green mother and father, that he might perhaps have a bundle of hay in one of the farms over there, that there might possibly ring in his ears the laughter of the young people, who cuddle in the doorway. That he possibly sleeps sometimes instead of dying.

THE MOUSE

Everywhere I go I bump into things, but I don't like doing this. I am well informed about traps. But this is not a trap, there is a continual reddish light here and it is mild. I can hear steps everywhere : the steps of human beings, of ducks, of sleepwalkers, of sons and daughters, there are many steps, those of the just, I can distinguish them all easily. Now and again a brighter light forces its way through the cracks and gives me ideas that I might possibly get out of here, but I do not submit to this idea, I refuse to consider it. I cherish rather fear, which is better since it demands from me no more than myself. I weigh it up and let it pass over me, from one side to the other, and thus I am soon able to distinguish the directions. There is little room here, but there are directions,

93

which are unlimited. They too are mild and they do not overwhelm me. When I move my ears I touch the wood on both sides of me; it is rough and I can smell it distinctly. But fear is better, it is grateful, and I imagine it as a big white flower, which sways to and fro in the morning wind (quite certainly on a stalk), and nervous people don't pick it. But the neighbours' children shout with joy at the sight of it, and the smell of it gets into their nostrils. My way home is lit for me, that much I do know, and I cannot miss the way, even if it isn't a proper way. But it is one of a kind. I feel like people who sit in a summerhouse, but I don't know why. I don't go into the house like they do, but I too have the network of the shadows on me. I don't go into the house because I can't any longer, but why should one always make a point of things which divide us? And why can't I go into the house? Because the doors are shut and all the big animals are all round the house, for this and other such external reasons? Or is it because I can't get out of here? But who knows if they can? Or if I can't? Let's leave the people in the summerhouse, I wish I had never even mentioned it. The neighbours' children are better, with their horses (it is true, one has a horse, even if he does live a long way away and hasn't much else), or a dog in a tree. They found it after it had been hanging there a long time and told us about it quite loudly. Or the mushroom gatherers, whose steps and talk I often hear, even if joylessly. And all the crowd of pilgrims! Almost everything goes too far. So let us rather stay where I am, as the well-known song has it. Not the sort of song the likes of us are ever likely to be able to hear. And for this reason the place too is suspect. Is it perhaps because it is a trap? Or because it isn't a trap? These are the sort of questions I ask myself. I don't want to ask for any pity. I don't want anybody, just for my sake, to rush into anything or even to slam a gate more firmly (that would embarrass me). I don't want anyone to approach me with wires and iron bars and try to save me; that would only cause unrest, and all the talk and rumour outside would pass unheard. And that would be a pity, even for the talk of the mushroom gatherers. Mushroom gatherers seldom listen to each other, and so their words rise up in the woods over the air into the old and wretched hideouts, words and syllables and even much less, alone and untraceable for ever. It is all due to the fact that they easily and yet never agree with each other, easily and yet never, and I do not intend to inflict it on them, or the words or the syllables or what comes out of it, fragments, rumours and not even the air, which deserts me. And so I am really here after all, listening, for my ears are sharp, and, in sounding the wood around me, I also sound the ice-fields, but I check nothing, I am merely present. And that is one of the advantages of my situation. Everyone else is all too easily suspected of wanting to check something, to get control of something, to master something. But not I. I am personally unaffected whether the ice breaks or not, and I hold the scales as long as I stay here. And I have no preferences, no special arenas, no streams surrounded by hills, no fanatics, I am the same to all. Anything which gives way one pace is just as important to me as two and three-layered blocks of houses which have in the end to be blown up. I bear them no ill-will for this, I have learnt how to control my

95

prejudices but I can only do so here. Who knows whether I might not set myself up as judge over the frozen lion, if I were outside, if I might not possibly begin to sniff at bridges, to decide on values or only take measurements; that itself arouses suspicion enough. The smell of wood would attract me, grooves from drilling, old lights or the sound of rutting stags. But not here. Dimensions here are so limited, that one can hardly call them dimensions, and they are beyond suspicion. This is neither a house nor a stable, it is neither a cheerful nor a sad surprise, and there is no need for a laurel or carnation wreath on the wall. No hides and no crow feathers nailed to the wall outside, not even a nail. And I am content for it to be so. There is no need for a bird to believe it just because of me, or for a flood to arise, or for the sun to rise, and that is as it should be. Laughter is heard without any reference to me. But how would it be, if I were to try to get out of here, if I were to take only one step in any direction? Everything would change. Either because I might find a way out or that I might discover that there is none : nothing would be the same any more. Exit or no exit, that is almost the same thing to me, as soon as I know. I could not be happy any more, my heart would be silent and still, even on the highest hill it would be a distant supposition, a poor, wretched thing. No, in my situation one should never consider or countenance exits, and never try to approach them with even the slightest movement. Let no plank rise or move, let no warmth from outside or any sweetness harm me and no fresh breath of air. Only then will the network of shadows on my back change and become my outline, my situation become my figure, but what of the torpor in which I am supposed to persist, the damp cold which envelops me? One should not utter beforehand one's every hope. One should imitate the bridges which, broken-down themselves, leave every step to those who only touch them lightly in passing, which start back at the mere sight of them and do not cross them; I know a number of them. It is incredible how many broken-down bridges there are, and yet still many possibilities of crossing the ice, detours, bends in the river, ways round the back, return routes, ways through the undergrowth, through the snow, past timber yards in plenty. A garden of snowdrops and oddments at the side of it, mushrooms, handkerchiefs, all considerately speared on sticks. Mushroom gatherers and will o' the wisp, all friends of mine, look thus far and no further! Keep in mind what you have within you. Move on, move on, stop ringing bells in the moonlight, and don't come running to me! And, you neighbour children, continue to pick the flowers and grow. Don't be as bold as you usually are and do not try to release me! For I don't want a mirror, or a pane of glass and not even a dark handful of water, which will reflect my image. Who knows, perhaps the secret of my joy lies in the fact that no one can find me.

97

DIALOGUES

NEVER AT ANY TIME

STUDENT *enters his attic room, closes the door behind him and walks up to the box of books behind the wooden post. He bends over it and begins to search.*

DWARF : Still hard at work?

STUDENT *absentmindedly* : Yes. *Only now does he notice the dwarf, who is standing on a box and wearing a tall green cap and, through the dormer window, can see over half the town.* What do you want here?

DWARF : Nothing. I am just looking over the town. Over to the green cupola of the castle. *Pointing to his cap.* I compare various shades of green. It is a thing one can go on doing all the time. Especially as this is a neighbourhood with plenty of gardens.

STUDENT, *bent over his book box, doesn't answer....*

DWARF : Every day between three and four. That gives my day its rhythms. It also makes me convinced that I actually stand here. And what about you?

STUDENT : I am looking for notes.

DWARF : Also between three and four?

STUDENT : Whenever I need them.

DWARF : And when do you need them?

STUDENT : When I don't find them down in here. I'm studying marine engineering.

DWARF : At what time?

STUDENT : Always.

DWARF : At no particular hour?

STUDENT : Always.

DWARF : What a pity. Otherwise we should meet more often up here.

STUDENT : That wouldn't be much good to me. I wouldn't get very far with that.

DWARF : Well, how far do you want to get?

STUDENT : As far as possible. On a ship—

DWARF : I often see some of them gliding past here, when I am comparing the green of the meadows with my hat—I could give you a recommendation—

STUDENT : I must finish my studies first. I want to get on.

DWARF : I also compare the green of the skyline with that of my hat. I've got connections, maybe.

STUDENT : But I must—

DWARF : You passed an examination only today.

STUDENT : Quite right. But how do you know—

DWARF : When I was comparing the green of the patina, with which the roof of the Technical Institute is gradually being covered, with the green of my hat, you were just receiving your Distinction.

STUDENT : That was my Intermediate Examination. Only after my Finals—

DWARF : You might like to consider applying to me.

STUDENT : I have a number of prospects—

DWARF : I shall be glad to recommend you.

STUDENT : But I must go home first. There I shall get married. And then—

DWARF : I am always here between three and four.

STUDENT : I have prospects in Germany and in America. The only question is—

DWARF : Always between three and four.

STUDENT : The question is—

DWARF : And I can always be of service to you

wherever there are shades of green. They are even quite common on ships.

STUDENT : Yes, on new ones, most likely.

DWARF : The sea has many of those.

STUDENT : But I shall not be building the sea but boats.

DWARF : Rivers!

STUDENT : It is not a question of river craft.

DWARF : I would like to bring into play for you all my connections with green!

STUDENT *stands upright, smoothing his hair back* : Here are my notes.

DWARF : You have no idea how much there is of it in the world, not only the green of the roofs and the gardens, but also that of the day, of the algae, of the sea bed, all discernible in comparisons—

STUDENT : I must go now!

DWARF · I could prove it to you, by my hat alone, by the tower of the Polish Church, by this bulbous spire—or by the green of the tree-tops near the Arsenal—

STUDENT *on his way out* : I'm afraid—

DWARF : If only you would come up and see me here from time to time—

STUDENT : It is my last term.

DWARF : Only between three and four—

STUDENT : I have lectures or practicals then. And when I am free, I must swot for my Finals and complete my sectional drawing of a ship.

DWARF : Or perhaps on your last day, on the day after your Finals. Between three and four.

STUDENT : I shall be packing my case then.

DWARF : It will be a hazy day, the fields will be grey,

the onions will be yellow and the roofs black. You'll always get a Distinction—

STUDENT : I hope to God I do!

DWARF : You've already said good-bye to your friends.

STUDENT : And then I am going to the station!

DWARF : There is one hour left, a good hour. You remember that there is a book box up here. Perhaps you could still find use for the odd one? You open the attic door. You go up to the book box, you bend down over it and search; no, you don't need any more books, all that is far behind you. You straighten up again—

STUDENT *impatiently, his notes in his hand* : Well?

DWARF : You look out over the attic window—You sigh—

STUDENT *standing at the open door* : I shan't sigh!

DWARF : I assure you you will. And then—

STUDENT : I must go now!

DWARF : Then I recommend to you the green of the sea.

The attic door slams shut.

DWARF *giggles and continues to gaze through the attic window over the town.*

BELVEDERE

DIRECTOR OF THE MUNICIPAL ZOO : Good morning!

DIRECTOR OF THE GALLERIES IN THE UPPER AND LOWER PALACE : And a good morning to you. I think I have had the pleasure of meeting you somewhere before?

ZOO DIRECTOR : Quite right. I have an appointment.

GALLERIES DIRECTOR : And what can I do for you?

ZOO DIRECTOR : I've come about the steers.

GALLERIES DIRECTOR *pondering* : About the steers?

ZOO DIRECTOR : Yes. The matter has been under discussion for years.

GALLERIES DIRECTOR : Steers—steers—

ZOO DIRECTOR : The white, Egyptian ones, if you don't mind my reminding you—

GALLERIES DIRECTOR : Steers?

ZOO DIRECTOR : The red-eyed ones!

GALLERIES DIRECTOR : A painting?

ZOO DIRECTOR : No. Steers.

GALLERIES DIRECTOR : Hm, I do seem to have heard something about them, but I can't think in what connection.

ZOO DIRECTOR : There was talk of accommodating them with you.

GALLERIES DIRECTOR : With me?

ZOO DIRECTOR : Yes.

GALLERIES DIRECTOR : Here? *He gestures towards the half-open window and the French garden outside, sloping upwards gently.*

ZOO DIRECTOR : That's right, between the Upper and Lower Palace.

GALLERIES DIRECTOR : How many?

ZOO DIRECTOR : The whole herd, about two hundred head.

GALLERIES DIRECTOR : That must have been before my time.

ZOO DIRECTOR : It was before my time, but at the beginning of yours. You negotiated with my predecessor.

GALLERIES DIRECTOR *shakes his head.*

ZOO DIRECTOR : The zoo was too small even then. In the meantime the herd has increased.

GALLERIES DIRECTOR : With the best will in the world, I just can't remember.

ZOO DIRECTOR *pressing the point* : The plan came to nothing then because we couldn't drive the herd through the cloister garden which abuts on the left, while the owner of the garden on the right also refused permission. In the meantime both these gardens have become public property.

GALLERIES DIRECTOR : A short time ago.

ZOO DIRECTOR : Yes. And the local authority would make no difficulties about helping the zoo.

GALLERIES DIRECTOR : I'm quite prepared to believe that.

ZOO DIRECTOR : Of course the herd could be driven in here with the greatest care for the gardens. We have plenty of skilled herdsmen.

GALLERIES DIRECTOR : And what about here?

ZOO DIRECTOR : Oh, they would stand head to head. But they would have room even now.

GALLERIES DIRECTOR : But—

ZOO DIRECTOR : If only it could be decided to run off the water from some of the stone basins, perhaps from all of them—

GALLERIES DIRECTOR : From all of them?

ZOO DIRECTOR : And drive the animals in. I think the edges of the basins are not too high.

GALLERIES DIRECTOR : I am not acquainted with the gait of white steers.

ZOO DIRECTOR : Oh, they are surprisingly agile. And, at the same time, remarkably quiet.

GALLERIES DIRECTOR : Oh, are they?

ZOO DIRECTOR : You need have no fear about your

view. You will still have a view through the half-open window—over the white heads and white horns, as over the mist of the morning and the glistening water, according to the season. You won't miss anything, all day long.

GALLERIES DIRECTOR : And what if I want to see the gravel and the fresh turf?

ZOO DIRECTOR : You won't want to once you have the sight of the white herd.

GALLERIES DIRECTOR : It is not a matter of my wishes.

ZOO DIRECTOR : It is certainly your business to keep the animals white.

GALLERIES DIRECTOR : My concern is the visitors to the galleries.

ZOO DIRECTOR : As long as the herd is white—

GALLERIES DIRECTOR : I don't care if the herd is white or black : what I wonder is what the people are to do who want to come down from the paintings in the Upper Palace to the sculptures in the Lower Palace, or those who need some peace on a Sunday morning and the feel of gravel under their feet, and to go from one to another?

ZOO DIRECTOR : They can walk on the road.

GALLERIES DIRECTOR : That is a detour. And, as I just said—

ZOO DIRECTOR : The question is really quite unimportant, because the Lower Palace is not going to be reserved for sculptures anyhow.

GALLERIES DIRECTOR : Not for sculptures?

ZOO DIRECTOR : Or at least only until the first rains come, until the first damp wind arises. Until, that is, it becomes necessary to drive the animals in.

GALLERIES DIRECTOR : Drive them in?

ZOO DIRECTOR : To maintain the whiteness of their

hide, that's very much to your purpose. So, if you would decide, at the first sign of rain or even as soon as the clouds form, that—

GALLERIES DIRECTOR : But the sculptures!

ZOO DIRECTOR : The galleries for sculpture are, as you know, better than I do, accommodated in the former stables. Alomst everything which today is called the Lower Palace's—

GALLERIES DIRECTOR : Not my rooms.

ZOO DIRECTOR : Your rooms wouldn't be touched. Your peace and quiet must be preserved even if only for the sake of the animals. It is important that they feel quiet above them, that their calm is reciprocated, out of two windows at least. And if there is not enough room in the galleries for the sculptures, you still have the Upper Palace. If the herd should increase here in your grounds—

GALLERIES DIRECTOR : I knew that's what you were leading up to!

ZOO DIRECTOR : The best thing for you and for the visitors. It would only be an emergency.

GALLERIES DIRECTOR : Which is certain to occur. As far as I can see, everything is being planned to meet this emergency. What, may I ask, can the animals do here but multiply?

ZOO DIRECTOR : Oh, they can paw the ground and stamp, and they can look glossy in surroundings appropriate to them.

GALLERIES DIRECTOR : In my limited experience—

ZOO DIRECTOR : You leave it to me.

GALLERIES DIRECTOR *firmly* : It won't be sufficient for them.

ZOO DIRECTOR : They are white steers, remember. And in the bright sunshine—

GALLERIES DIRECTOR : Hardly in bright sunshine, and even less so when a damp wind gets up or at the first vague signs of cloud.

ZOO DIRECTOR : They are red-eyed ones.

GALLERIES DIRECTOR : What advantage is that? And in such overcrowding?

ZOO DIRECTOR : We'll wait and see.

GALLERIES DIRECTOR : I will but you can't.

ZOO DIRECTOR : I am quite convinced—

GALLERIES DIRECTOR : Who's going to feed the animals?

ZOO DIRECTOR : From the outset the zoo and the local authority will assume part of the responsibility for the animals.

GALLERIES DIRECTOR : But what of the inhabitants of the neighbouring houses, who have rented them for the view over the gardens?

ZOO DIRECTOR : At the first sight of the white herd they will realise what they have missed hitherto; what has made the gardens for years seem empty to them, the birds' singing only sneaking and underhand, and the gravel paths lustreless. At the easy movement of the herd they will again feel what has long been hidden from them and what is truly worthwhile.

GALLERIES DIRECTOR : But the smell of dung—

ZOO DIRECTOR : Yes, that's part of it.

GALLERIES DIRECTOR : And who's going to cart the dung away?

ZOO DIRECTOR : I have already told you that, in the beginning, the zoo will take its share in looking after the animals. And you needn't worry about later. When once the drovers and stockmen have moved in to surrounding streets, the dung can easily—

GALLERIES DIRECTOR : The drovers and stockmen?

ZOO DIRECTOR : The ones you appoint, of course.

GALLERIES DIRECTOR : I appoint?

ZOO DIRECTOR : So long as the inhabitants of the neighbouring houses can prove that they are prepared and capable to take on such jobs, they could quite well go on living in their houses.

GALLERIES DIRECTOR : They will be pleased to hear that!

ZOO DIRECTOR : Yes, they will, won't they. And you can take over the supervision—

GALLERIES DIRECTOR : I thought as much.

ZOO DIRECTOR : You are well acquainted with them. Your efforts on behalf of the treasures in the galleries are well known. If you were instead to turn your efforts to the herd—

GALLERIES DIRECTOR : Instead?

ZOO DIRECTOR : It will be accepted. And not only accepted. The importance attached to the white steers—

GALLERIES DIRECTOR : And heifers.

ZOO DIRECTOR : The importance attached to the whole herd will equal that attached formerly to the sculptures and paintings in the galleries, on certain Sunday mornings, when one didn't know whether it was the sun or the shadow. One will compare the elegance and the tints of the antlers, and go and watch the calves in the roomy galleries.

GALLERIES DIRECTOR : I wonder why all that cannot be done in the zoo.

ZOO DIRECTOR : For the reasons I have mentioned. And one more thing.

GALLERIES DIRECTOR : The galleries would be prepared, out of the proceeds from the sale of one or other item of sculpture to make a contribution to its extension—

ZOO DIRECTOR: That is impossible. Otherwise I would not be sitting here—

GALLERIES DIRECTOR: But why?

ZOO DIRECTOR: You know that steers react to certain colours—?

GALLERIES DIRECTOR: Where is there any red in the Zoo?

ZOO DIRECTOR: They are Egyptian steers. Red-eyed ones!

GALLERIES DIRECTOR: What difference does that make?

ZOO DIRECTOR: They get angry at the sight of another colour.

GALLERIES DIRECTOR: Of another colour?

ZOO DIRECTOR: They are very sensitive to green. And while the green of the hedges here is quickly eaten, and the green of the turf quickly trampled under-foot—

GALLERIES DIRECTOR: And the green of the roofs?

ZOO DIRECTOR: Easily painted over in another colour; it is also necessary for the sake of the other animals in the zoo to keep green limited.

GALLERIES DIRECTOR: And how are the roofs here to be painted over?

ZOO DIRECTOR: I leave that to you. After all, your long experience with painting and your delight in shades of colour, you know—

GALLERIES DIRECTOR: Yes, I know.

ZOO DIRECTOR *rises*: It's striking twelve.

GALLERIES DIRECTOR: And what about the green of the church towers, of the bordering gardens and roofs of the nearby houses?

ZOO DIRECTOR: I leave all that to you. As far as the public garden on the west side is concerned, it will soon be turned into a feeding place for the steers. And the cloister garden on the eastern side—

GALLERIES DIRECTOR: I have no control over that.

ZOO DIRECTOR: Oh, that'll be sorted out in time. And, by the way, it will be advisable to have the ringing of the monastery bells stopped. And not only monastery bells, but all bell-ringing, all bell-like sounds within a wide radius.

GALLERIES DIRECTOR: That is quite a large area.

ZOO DIRECTOR: The herd has got its own bells, and any others would only confuse them.

GALLERIES DIRECTOR: This garden here was laid out because it was desired, from the most distant towers, from the churches in the villages on the other side of the river, which don't even belong to the town—

ZOO DIRECTOR: The herd's bells will make up for everything—amply. And at last people will know where the sound comes from. None other than you will be able to explain that to the vicars and sacristans of even the most distant villages.

GALLERIES DIRECTOR: Surely you don't mean to say —that I—

ZOO DIRECTOR: No one will be able to say it better than you: 'Please stop all bell-ringing. It confuses the animals.'

GALLERIES DIRECTOR: I think it is much more likely that the slope of this garden will confuse the herd, that and the shrubs which have such resemblance to human beings.

ZOO DIRECTOR: There are even more precipitous slopes and even more human-looking shrubbery.

GALLERIES DIRECTOR: To come back to the question

of the green, what colours are you thinking of to replace it?

ZOO DIRECTOR : Red, black, blue or yellow, as I have already said—

GALLERIES DIRECTOR : My pleasure in shades of colour.

ZOO DIRECTOR : And the movement of the herd, to which you have to conform.

GALLERIES DIRECTOR : How am I to—

ZOO DIRECTOR : When you see the animals moving close together past the sphinxes along the broad pathways, your delight will overcome everything.

GALLERIES DIRECTOR : The question is, how am I to make clear to the children who used to play in this garden—

ZOO DIRECTOR : They will be thrilled about the steers.

GALLERIES DIRECTOR : And what about their grand-mothers?

ZOO DIRECTOR : They will share the delight of their grandchildren. They will think they are recalling a long-lost memory, while the memory of the future will rise up in the grandchildren. No one who does no more than merely glance at these white backs will be able to withstand the attraction to look for what he is set on and to see it at last; not gravel paths, shrubbery, sculptures, paintings and unmentionable things seen in insufficient lighting, no : broad white backs in the sun, heads, antlers, the whole herd— steers!

GALLERIES DIRECTOR : And when is that to be?

ZOO DIRECTOR : Soon.

GALLERIES DIRECTOR : You will notify me?

ZOO DIRECTOR : Yes, even if I myself don't come any more—

GALLERIES DIRECTOR : So I had better begin to move out.

ZOO DIRECTOR : It is agreed that you are to be compensated.

GALLERIES DIRECTOR : And what about my post here as Director of these galleries?

ZOO DIRECTOR : That will be extended to cover the neighbouring street blocks, the roofs and towers and the neighbouring gardens.

GALLERIES DIRECTOR : But those are only temporary measures.

ZOO DIRECTOR : Which, if I were in your position, I would consider attractive.

GALLERIES DIRECTOR : And what is going to happen in the end? When all the bells have stopped ringing, when all the gardens have been stripped bare, and when even the green of the surrounding towers and cupolas has disappeared, when all those unwilling to be turned into stockmen and drovers have given up their houses, and when steers push their way in amongst stone steps and dried-up water fountains, lit by the sun? When the easily shifting frontiers between their own bodies become the only frontiers still visible from here?

ZOO DIRECTOR : The windows here are to stay half-open, as they have been just now.

GALLERIES DIRECTOR : And what about me? Me? When all the galleries up there and down here are to be cleared of sculptures and paintings, and when the time comes when I can no longer of an evening get ready to go and spend one quiet moment surveying the treasures?

ZOO DIRECTOR : All you will be concerned about, as I am today, will be the whiteness of the steers.

III

GALLERIES DIRECTOR : And what about the evenings?

ZOO DIRECTOR : Then as well. By then you will probably be half-blinded. All those who have regarded for years the stimulating whiteness of the herd grow blind in time.

GALLERIES DIRECTOR : And shall I go blind?

ZOO DIRECTOR *already on his way out* : Yes.

GALLERIES DIRECTOR : To come back once more to the subject of green : there are certain moments, as occur sometimes before a thunderstorm, when the sky assumes a slightly green colouring. Evenings too, but less often.

ZOO DIRECTOR : It would be a dreadful shock for the herd, perhaps a sign to rush at everything within range.

GALLERIES DIRECTOR : But how—

ZOO DIRECTOR : Oh, you'll know how to prevent that !

GALLERIES DIRECTOR : I don't think that my delight in shades of colour in a case like this—

ZOO DIRECTOR *has already gone.*

GALLERIES DIRECTOR : My experience of pictures extending over many years—*steps up to the window and looks up to the sky.* Turn green !

A child calls to another. Birds chirp. The sky is blue and there are some white clouds to be seen.

FIRST TERM

STUDENT *she is no longer young* : I wondered if I could find accommodation here.

PORTRESS *she is no longer young either* : Accommodation?

STUDENT: There is supposed to be a hostel here for students who don't come from this neighbourhood.

PORTRESS: Our hostel is full up, I mean—

STUDENT: I have a recommendation from my parish.

PORTRESS: Where do you come from?

STUDENT: Two hours by train from here, to the north-east. You won't know my name. But our vicar—

PORTRESS: How long are you thinking of staying?

STUDENT: As long as possible.

PORTRESS: As long as possible?

STUDENT: I should have said: two or three years. No longer.

PORTRESS: The hostel is open.

STUDENT: Open? Didn't you say just now—

PORTRESS: That it is full?

STUDENT: Yes.

PORTRESS: Quite right. It is full.

STUDENT: I don't understand. There is the notice above the door.

PORTRESS: Oh, yes, we have to put that up.

STUDENT: And it is in the telephone book under the entry 'Hostel for external students'.

PORTRESS *who sits suddenly upright*: Open in the temporary sense of the word, but full up in the permanent sense.

STUDENT *thoughtfully, frowning*: You mean—

PORTRESS: And can be filled only in this sense.

STUDENT *in a lively tone*: So I could stay after all?

PORTRESS: Yes. As I said just now—

STUDENT: Does my vicar know of this condition?

PORTRESS: I am afraid, in vicarages two hours' train journey to the north-east—but won't you come in?

STUDENT : I want to know first what you mean by 'permanently'.

PORTRESS : That is a difficult thing to discuss with the door open.

STUDENT : Perhaps I should have to be a perpetual first-term student?

PORTRESS : Well, at least in the term in which you happen to be.

STUDENT : In my case that would be the first. And stay in the same faculty?

PORTRESS : In the one you have chosen, yes.

STUDENT : That is the same one. *Thoughtfully*. I don't think that my vicar—I haven't got the fare now to go back home again and ask him.

PORTRESS : I am quite sure that your vicar—

STUDENT : Our vicar wants me to finish my studies and to open a practice in our village.

PORTRESS : I don't want to urge you unduly, but it is beginning to rain. If only you would make up your mind soon—

STUDENT : Wouldn't I have to go on hearing the same lectures?

PORTRESS : You would get used to that.

STUDENT : You know what I mean, always the same one?

PORTRESS : You know that before God a thousand years are like a single day.

STUDENT *winding a scarf round her head, hesitatingly* : Yes.

PORTRESS : Well, as many lectures as are usual on this day. Five or six, some of those who lodge here have in addition tutorials or practicals.

STUDENT : But I am not likely to have any. First term, you know!

PORTRESS : No. Even less so since this is only the second day. But there are advantages in this. You will be able to get about in the open quite a lot. In the early afternoon you will be able to go for walks in the little park near here.

STUDENT *looking upwards* : Always under this milky sky in the light drizzle?

PORTRESS : There are people who like drizzle.

STUDENT : Oh, of course. At home, I always—

PORTRESS : And towards evening you will be able to see through the lit-up windows opposite the same children coming home from school in the afternoon. The boy will sit down at the piano. And the girl will—

STUDENT *dreamily* : And then it will begin to rain more violently and grow dark. I shall open the window. And the slight smell of smoke—

PORTRESS : Will always hang about in the air.

STUDENT : It really is raining much more heavily.

PORTRESS : Would you like to come on in? There is a fire, even in the hall.

STUDENT *without even putting a foot inside* : All fitted with blue tiles?

PORTRESS : Yes.

STUDENT : It really is very nice. I just wonder if my vicar—

PORTRESS : White curtains in every room.

STUDENT : I wonder, if my vicar could see what it is like here—

PORTRESS : And central heating, of course, flowers and built-in cupboards.

STUDENT : He has always been very concerned about my welfare.

PORTRESS : He has no need to worry any more about it.

STUDENT *thoughtfully* : No.

PORTRESS : Well, you see.

STUDENT : I am still wondering : what about Christmas?

PORTRESS : Oh, it is always near without actually coming. Besides, recently—*smiling*—when we still used to count in years, it gradually became a stranger and stranger thing.

STUDENT *to herself* : It is near.

PORTRESS : Yes. Always this milky sky presaging snow clouds. But it isn't snowing. The shop windows aren't decorated yet, but they will be soon.

STUDENT : I had intended to go home for Christmas.

PORTRESS : You wouldn't want that.

STUDENT : Not want that?

PORTRESS : Since you've just come from home. This day has also the advantage that it isn't so far away from summer. It is even the day on which summer develops properly for the first time. You have home, fields, meadows and hay in your mind—without admittedly their disturbing you.

STUDENT : There are not many fields where we are. But it is true : I was indeed just thinking of that.

PORTRESS : Everything is near.

STUDENT : Yes.

PORTRESS : What are you still pondering?

STUDENT : Our vicar—

PORTRESS : You will never run into the danger of disappointing him. Your vicar—

STUDENT : Shall I always wear this blue hat? *Puts her hand up to her head.*

PORTRESS : Of course. And always meet children, when you are out for a walk, with similar hats.

STUDENT : Meet children, that's marvellous.

PORTRESS : Nice, cheerful children. They run past you laughing, brush against your handbags with theirs as they run laughing past in the dusk.

STUDENT : Oh, marvellous.

PORTRESS : Come in.

STUDENT *hesitating, her foot already on the threshhold* : But what if I were to want to live somewhere else?

PORTRESS : Somewhere else? I assume you have no relatives in the town?

STUDENT : What if I am unable in spite of all to make up my mind?

PORTRESS : Well, the rain which is now falling on your coat will very soon turn into snow. From today onwards everything will begin to take its course with frenzied speed : Christmas will come and pass again just as quickly, summer will come and will not stay for a moment.

STUDENT : But I shall be able to finish my studies?

PORTRESS : The ten terms will pass quicker than a morning here, then a few pleasant and not too difficult inaugural lectures you have to attend.

STUDENT : And I shall be able to take over the practice in my native town?

PORTRESS : Yes, much more likely than you will let your hands fall, exhausted, weak, for ever, than you return here from your little walk in the drizzle, to drink a cup of tea and dry your clothes.

STUDENT : But our vicar?

PORTRESS : Your vicar, who lives only two hours' train journey away—

STUDENT : Yes, always.

PORTRESS : Your vicar will have been dead ages ago then. What are you still undecided about?

117

STUDENT : Oh, everything. *She withdraws her foot, the door of the hostel for external students is slammed shut and the snow begins to fall in big, watery flakes.*

SUNDAY DUTY

STEWARDESS OF THE LONDON-JOHANNESBURG PAS-SENGER AIRCRAFT *comes slowly along the dimly-lit corridor of the clinic for nervous disorders and knocks at the door of the assistant physician* : Good evening.

DOCTOR : Is it as late as that? I thought it might be —the morning passed today almost imperceptibly into evening. Those who are not compelled to keep to fixed mealtimes could easily confuse day and night.

STEWARDESS : It's getting on for four.

DOCTOR : I had just opened the window to feed the sparrows.

STEWARDESS : Yes, I saw you. I came up across the park.

DOCTOR : But they weren't very hungry. It is damp enough today for them to be able to find their own food.

STEWARDESS : Yes.

DOCTOR : I am glad you came. I don't like days when one is on duty and yet feels off duty.

STEWARDESS : That's why I'm here too.

DOCTOR : You are giving me relief from myself, as it were. Come and sit down here. Oh, forgive me, I forgot to introduce myself—

STEWARDESS : I know you.

DOCTOR *cheerfully* : By sight, probably. I seem to remember having seen you, too, in the corridor some-where. You were waiting for someone.

STEWARDESS : I was waiting for you.

DOCTOR : For me?

STEWARDESS : It was a Sunday, like today, and you were on duty. It was a brighter day. Then you were called away. *Hesitantly.* It is a pity.

DOCTOR *impatiently* : And now you've found me.

STEWARDESS : It was better flying weather then.

DOCTOR : You are the patient who was transferred to me. You were asked to come today at four o'clock? *Looking at the clock.*

STEWARDESS : I'm on duty on the London-Johannesburg route.

DOCTOR : Our town lies a bit off that route.

STEWARDESS : But it lies on mine.

DOCTOR : Our clinic lies in turn rather far from the airport.

STEWARDESS : I can get here quite easily. At this time of day—

DOCTOR : It isn't four yet.

STEWARDESS : And at this height?

DOCTOR : Which height?

STEWARDESS : Of the moment when you fling open the window and feel off duty without actually being so.

DOCTOR : And how high is that moment?

STEWARDESS : Atlantic height. About four thousand above sea level.

DOCTOR : That's not a very precise indication.

STEWARDESS *eagerly* : I could tell you more exactly. Latitude—

DOCTOR : Thank you. The moment is not at all appropriate for me, and the clouds over the isolation wing are passing too rapidly for my liking. The sky here is alternately high and low. The sun seems as if it is shining and then again as if it were not.

STEWARDESS : The height exact to a thousandth part.

DOCTOR : Too inappropriate for such exactitude.

STEWARDESS *more insistently* : We passed over Southampton half an hour ago.

DOCTOR *smiling for a moment* : We shan't be landing there, I suppose?

STEWARDESS *shakes her head*..

DOCTOR : Don't bother any more. I shall be working for some years here yet. And then not even the sparrows will know me, let alone—

STEWARDESS : Everything can be checked and determined.

DOCTOR : Of what use is it, if I myself don't determine anything?

STEWARDESS : For that very reason.

DOCTOR : What do you want?

STEWARDESS *uneasy* : I have not been in this job very long.

DOCTOR : Are you afraid?

STEWARDESS : Recently, yes.

DOCTOR : How long ago?

STEWARDESS : Since August 23rd.

DOCTOR : Since August 23rd?

STEWARDESS : A Sunday. I was on duty.

DOCTOR : I expect I was as well.

STEWARDESS : And ever since then I have been afraid when I had Sunday duty.

DOCTOR : And never on other occasions?

STEWARDESS : No. And even then not all day long. Only from three till six.

DOCTOR : That is a comparatively short time.

STEWARDESS *becomes hesitant again* : It is always.

DOCTOR *kindly* : What about the morning? Or the evening? Weekdays?

STEWARDESS *shakes her head.*

DOCTOR : How nice!

STEWARDESS *imploringly* : You know what Sundays from three till six means. How long it is till four.

DOCTOR : What good is that to you?

STEWARDESS : It is the duty arrangement we have. Every third Sunday, sometimes every other Sunday. It changes according to a definite plan.

DOCTOR : You soon worked that out.

STEWARDESS : People who are afraid—

DOCTOR : And what about before August 23rd?

STEWARDESS : Oh, I had time then. All day weekdays and also Sunday mornings. We took off at three o'clock.

DOCTOR : Were you afraid then?

STEWARDESS : Not at first. But only when we had climbed to four thousand did I notice that it was Sunday. And that we were flying in a direction which was not a very hopeful one in order to get into a Monday.

DOCTOR : Yes, I know that feeling.

STEWARDESS : Shortly before four I was ordered to take emergency measures.

DOCTOR : And when—

STEWARDESS : It wasn't till after six that we lost height and came down. On a mud bank by the shore. The plane was on fire.

DOCTOR : After six o'clock on August 23rd.

STEWARDESS : You put on your hat and coat and went into town.

DOCTOR : Maybe I did. I can't remember any more.

STEWARDESS : But I do.

DOCTOR : Why have you come?

STEWARDESS : Because I helped to drag eleven passengers from the flames but not the twelfth. I pushed my way out before him.

DOCTOR : And ever since—

STEWARDESS : Ever since I've been looking for you.

DOCTOR : The treatment here—

STEWARDESS *quickly*: I wanted to ask you to take my duty for me from three till six.

DOCTOR : When?

STEWARDESS : Only on those Sundays when you are on duty and feed the sparrows, days on which no one comes. *As the doctor hesitates.* That does not happen often for you but for me it is always so.

DOCTOR : What does your duty consist of?

STEWARDESS : From three to four it consists of uneasiness. And later it consists of fear. At six I will step in dependably.

DOCTOR *thoughtfully*: Haven't I done duty for you on occasions already?

STEWARDESS : Partly. Now I am asking you.

DOCTOR : And how long for?

STEWARDESS : Until I succeed in letting the twelfth passenger go out ahead of me, until I can gain control of the moment and get these three hours done away with. *As he still hesitates.* Until I can face the mud and the fire, fresh as a child awaking out of a deep sleep who can still see the angels. It is not for nothing that we have the same duty hours.

DOCTOR *nods to her*: We don't want them to be for nothing.

She has gone.

POEMS

WINTER ANSWER

The world is composed of the substance
which calls for consideration :
no eyes any more
to see the white meadows with,
no ears to hear
the fluttering birds in the branches.
Grandmother, where have your lips gone,
to taste for us the grasses,
and who will smell for us the extent of the sky,
whose cheeks are rubbed raw
on the village walls today?
Is it not a gloomy forest
which we have happened on?
No, grandmother, it's not a gloomy forest,
I know this, for I have lived long
with the children on its fringes,
and it is not even a forest.

WALK

Since the world emerges from distances,
staircases and marshlands,
and what is bearable becomes suspect,
then do not admit
that the magpies start up behind your sheds

and plunge down again with glittering wings into the
    shining pond,
that the smoke from your dwellings rises up
in front of the woods,
let us rather wait
until the golden foxes
appear before us in the snow.

CORRESPONDENCE

If the mail were to come at nighttime
and if the moon were to push insults
under the door :
they would appear like angels
in their white raiment
and would stand, still and silent, in the hall.

DEDICATION

I will write you all no letters,
but I would find it easy to die with you.
We would slide gently down the moons
and if the first resting place were to be still in woollen
    hearts,
the second would already find us with the wolves and
    the raspberry canes
and the non-assuaging fire, and at the third, ah, then
    I would have
gone through the thin, falling clouds with their scanty
    mosses
and the poor milling throng of stars, which we
    traversed so easily,
and be in your heaven with you all.

INSTRUCTIONS

Take desires
by the edges,
wrap the earth in wax,
build ramparts,
go on turning leaves.
And with hollow roses
may think
new helpers have come,
heroes, complainants,
adventurers.
It is said they are friends.

END OF THE WRITTEN RECORD

Thus none will know
of our panted breath
as we ran over the bridge,
and they will never know
what lies behind us :
the faint characters,
the truncated suns.
The entrance halls of hospitals
are silent.

NEAR LINZ

I with the day on my heels
and the rough, uneven country roads.
Listen to the jolting !
Do not overtake me, my day,
but stay close to my heels.

BIBLIOGRAPHY

(A) ORIGINAL TEXTS

1. *Die Größere Hoffnung,* Frankfurt (Fischer), 1948.
   (*The Greater Hope*—Novel.)
2. *Knöpfe,* Frankfurt (Fischer), 1961.
   (*Buttons*—Radio Play, first broadcast 1953.)
3. *Der Gefesselte,* Frankfurt (Fischer), 1954.
   (*The Bound Man*—Short Stories.)
4. *Zu keiner Stunde,* Frankfurt (Fischer), 1957.
   (*Never at any Time*—Dialogues.)
*5. 'Die Silbermünze,' Stuttgart (Reclam), 1959.
   ('The Silver Coin'—Short Story, written 1956.)
*6. 'Nichts und das Boot,' Paderborn (Schöningh), 1959.
   ('Naught and the boat'—Short Story, written 1951.)
7. *Besuch im Pfarrhaus,* Frankfurt (Fischer), 1961.
   (*A Visit to the Vicarage*—Radio Play & Dialogues.)
8. *Wo ich Wohne,* Frankfurt (Fischer), 1961.
   (*Where I Live*—Short Stories, Dialogues, Poems.)
9. *Eliza Eliza*, Frankfurt (Fischer), 1965.
   ('Eliza Eliza'—Short Stories.)
†10. 'Der junge Leutnant', Oxford (Pergamon), 1966.
   ('The Young Lieutenant'—Short Story.)
(In addition to the above, some dozen poems, not

*—Aichinger herself retains the copyright of these stories.
†—See C. 4 below.

yet collected into a volume, have appeared in the periodicals *Akzente* and *Die Neve Rundschau* (1955, 1959, 1960).)

(B) TRANSLATIONS IN ENGLISH
1. *The Bound Man and Other Stories,* London (Secker and Warburg), 1955.
   (Translated by E. Mosbacher. American edition: New York (Noonday Press), 1956.)
2. 'Where I Live', *Shenandoah Review* XII (1960).
   (Translated by A. L. Lancaster.)
3. 'Story in Reverse', New York (Bantam Books), 1961.
   (Edited by H. Steinhauer.)
4. 'Herod's Children', New York (Atheneum Books), 1964.
   (Translated by C. Schaeffer.)
5. 'Story in Reverse', Harmondsworth (Penguin), 1964.
   (In: *German Short Stories* (Parallel Text edition), translated by C. Levenson.)
6. 'The Young Lieutenant', *Mundus Artium* I (1967).
   (Translated by J. C. Alldridge.)
7. 'Angels in the Night', London (Oswald Wolff), 1968.
   (In: *German Narrative Prose*, Vol. III. Translated by E. Mosbacher.)

In Preparation:
1. 'Never at any Time' and 'Eliza Eliza'.
   (Translated by J. C. Alldridge.)
2. 'Where I Live'.
   (Translated by Alice Weinreich.)

(C) CRITICAL WORKS

(Apart from very brief references in anthologies of short stories which print some of her work, critical material on Aichinger is almost non-existent. Her position in contemporary German literature finds passing mention in the first three works listed below, and is treated more fully in the fourth on this list, which is devoted entirely to her.)

1. H. M. Waidson (ed.), *German Short Stories*, Cambridge (University Press), 1957.
2. *Begegnung von A bis Z* (English Introduction by R. Samuel), Melbourne (Heinemann), 1964.
3. Hinton Thomas (ed.) *Seventeen Modern German Stories*, Oxford (University Press), 1965.
4. J. C. Alldridge (ed.), Ilse Aichinger : *Selected Short Stories and Dialogues*, Oxford (Pergamon), 1966.
   (This volume printed for the first time, with the author's permission, the story 'Der junge Leutnant'.)

The best critical material in German:

5. 'Die deutsche Kurzgeschichte der Jahrhundertmitte', *Der Deutschunterricht* IX (Heft 1), 1957.
6. K. Nonnemann (ed.), *Schriftsteller der Gegenwart—Deutsche Literatur*, Olten & Freiburg (Walter), 1963.
7. A. Hildebrandt, 'Zu Ilse Aichingers Gedichten', *Literatur und Kritik* Nr. 23, Salzburg (Otto Müller), 1968.